First published 2017 by Boxtree
an imprint of Pan Macmillan
20 New Wharf Road, London N1 9RR
Associated companies throughout the world
www.panmacmillan.com

ISBN 978-0-7522-6648-0

1 3 5 7 9 8 6 4 2

A CIP catalogue record for this book is available from the British Library.

Typeset by Birdy Book Design
Printed and bound in Italy

Visit **www.panmacmillan.com** to read more about all our books
and to buy them. You will also find features, author interviews and
news of any author events, and you can sign up for e-newsletters
so that you're always first to hear about our new releases.

THE SECRET LIFE OF 4, 5 AND 6 YEAR OLDS

What Little People Can Tell Us About Big People

TERESA WATKINS
with PROFESSOR PAUL HOWARD-JONES

BOXTREE

contents

Introduction   1

Making friends   13

Little grown-ups   39

Language and the art of persuasion   61

Feelings and what to do with them   83

Girls and boys   105

Resisting temptation   129

Learning to lie, learning to love   143

How to win at winning and losing   163

If at first you don't succeed . . .   181

And finally . . .   189

Appendix 1: The making of *The
Secret Life of 4, 5 and 6 Year Olds*   193

Appendix 2: *Do* try this at home   198

Acknowledgements   202

introduction

Anyone who's ever spent time around young children knows how funny the things they say can be. As they get to grips with the surprising new world around them, the things they see and hear often get jumbled up and put back together in an order that is completely their own. And sometimes it's as if they are uncovering some deep truth about life. When my children were that age, like many other parents, I wrote down things they said because their take on the world was so idiosyncratic and funny. 'How long does a cloud take to get to America?' 'Maybe both of us are not born yet and both of us are dreaming?' 'Do they have big bosoms in the art gallery?'

Joe: Today I'm a swordfish.

Similarly, many of us will have had that experience of walking past a doorway and overhearing a fragment of conversation in which for a moment a whole other reality is glimpsed. As soon as we put our head round the door our presence changes everything and the mysterious realm of children without adults melts away.

The Secret Life of 4, 5 and 6 Year Olds began with the hunch that it would be interesting to put our heads round the door for a little while longer.

It was partly based on personal experience. I had often wished I could follow my children across the threshold of nursery. Which parent hasn't wondered who their child is when they're not around – whether they're loud or quiet, rough or gentle, the centre of attention or sitting on the sidelines? So much of that curious process of them becoming the person they will grow into happens when we are not around.

But as we sat on the first day of filming, huddled behind bookshelves, listening through our headphones, we realized our hunch was truer than we had imagined – it was enthralling. It was clear that you don't have to be a parent or even especially interested in children to find people at this age fascinating.

What do you want to be when you grow up? Emily: Jelly maker. Pencil sharpener. Toy maker.

Within minutes of the children meeting each other, we saw them hoarding bricks, forming raiding parties for trucks and aeroplanes, two boys butting up against each other like stags until one came out on top. There were pecking orders, alliances, an in-group and an out-group. Their interactions were sophisticated, complex and dramatic. As we watched, we found ourselves identifying very quickly with individual children, picking out the one who most reminded us of ourselves, as adults. And we began to realize how much of who we are today connects back to who we were at four years old.

As we watched one girl's struggle to make a friend, a boy becoming ostracized for trying to get his own way and another boy asking everyone to come to his party, we recognized these impulses as part of our everyday lives. We often saw behaviour that collapsed the distance between the adult world and childhood. Whether the children were hurling insults, pushing and shoving, or throwing a tantrum, these things we saw in the playground made us think of the same behaviour we'd seen in boardrooms, bars and bus queues all our lives.

After all, who hasn't felt the four-year-old rise up when there's a plate of biscuits in a meeting and just one chocolate one left? Or when someone gets served before you at the bar? Or even on the first day at a new job, when you don't know anyone yet?

However, we weren't fully prepared for the genuine chord the show struck with the viewing public; everyone from adults who simply enjoyed watching the children's antics to people who identified with one child or another, or who remembered the feeling of being that age themselves. We heard from teachers who liked seeing children as fully rounded, complex characters, from parents who felt liberated from their own anxieties as they watched, and even from children and young viewers who relished seeing themselves reflected back in the unfolding stories with something approaching nostalgia.

Again and again we heard how joyous it was to see the rich, complex and surprising worlds of these children, and how much it made people think about their own behaviour and lives.

What's the bravest thing you've ever done? Arran: I tried a green bean.

Why four, five and six-year-olds?

The Secret Life of 4, 5 and 6 Year Olds had its genesis in developmental science. Scientists interested in child development see four years old as a pivotal age because so many of the social skills that we need for adult life are laid down around this time.

Back in the 1960s, Professor Walter Mischel devised his famous Marshmallow Test. In it, children were offered a treat by a scientist in a white coat and told they could eat

one treat straight away or receive two if they waited ten minutes. When they followed up years later, Mischel found that the ability of the four-year-old to delay gratification and to hold out for a bigger reward over the instant gratification of a smaller one had turned out to be a very strong predictor of their future success.

This doesn't mean that you can determine who a person is going to be at four years old, of course. But it's clear that there are very real connections between who we are then and the adults we become.

As the idea for *The Secret Life of 4, 5 and 6 Year Olds* took root we collaborated with a number of scientists, including Professor Paul Howard-Jones of Bristol University, whose specialism is the neuroscience of learning – in other words, how our brains learn to learn. In the programme, we had scientists observing the play at all times, partly to ensure that the environment was safe and positive for the children and that our challenges were grounded in scientific research, but also because we knew how much insight they would bring to the action as it unfolded. There have been plenty of television programmes that have shown us kids saying and doing the funniest things. But we wanted to know *why*, to try and understand what was going on inside their heads. I am pleased to have the opportunity in this book to include more of the science behind the behaviour of children, thanks to Professor Howard-Jones. For him, the programme was a rare opportunity to observe children up close at this critical age.

At four years old children are on the cusp of two worlds, with one foot still firmly embedded in their home life, the other stepping out into the world of their peers, of new adults, school and formal education. It is a threshold into the social world – a world that will ultimately give them independence – and once across the threshold there is no coming back. This 'stepping out' coincides with an explosion in language skills, giving us fresh insight into their internal worlds just as they begin to project their own imaginative thoughts and ideas onto the adult world around them.

Why is this age so interesting?

At birth we have roughly as many neurons as there are stars in the Milky Way. The number of connections per neuron is about 2,500. By age two or three it's about 15,000 connections per neuron. And as children learn, so their experience and interpretation of the world comes to be reflected in these connections. At four years old a child's social experience in the playground is rapidly wiring their brain, with adult and peer interactions influencing which connections are made and which are 'pruned'.

Brain development does not stop after childhood, but early brain development, and the experiences that influence it, are the foundation upon which later skills build. This is what makes this period of child development so important. And so fascinating.

Developmentally there is an awful lot going on at four years old. Alongside their widening vocabulary, they are learning a whole range of social skills that will form the foundation for their adult lives – everything from sharing to making friends, to developing empathy. And in a broader sense they are moving from a world view in which they are firmly at the centre of their own universe to one in which they recognize that other people have thoughts and feelings that may be different to their own. This is a huge shift, and it takes time to understand that other people have their own perspective and to master this brave new world. Indeed many of us are still on that journey.

The sheer amount of new learning taking place at this time explains why we see a kind of 'one step forward, two steps back' mechanism played out repeatedly in the playground; we are literally watching as children's brains are being wired and rewired. What a comfort to know that when your child throws another tantrum or celebrates another win by rubbing their opponents faces in it, this is simply because the new wiring isn't quite in place yet.

We realized that to fully grasp the significance of these developmental stages we needed to look at a broader age range of children. And so we recreated the same conditions in subsequent programmes for five and six-year-olds and the differences have been fascinating, as Professor Howard-Jones explains: 'The average four-year-old is struggling just to get through the day without losing it. It can take all their concentration to control their impulses and refrain from behaviour that damages their friendships – like refusing to share or being aggressive.

'By the age of five, children are developing a strong sense of one-to-one friendship, but working hard to avoid emotional chaos in their social life as they constantly make and break up with each other.

'At six years old, one-to-one friendships are more stable and children are juggling them with their desire to be part of a group.'

Amelia-Rose: She's not very nice, is 'er? 'Er needs to learn some manners.

Understanding a little of what's going on in the brain helps illuminate so much of the children's behaviour. Take grudges, for example. What are they and why do we hold on to them so fiercely? One day we watched as a four-year-old girl made the tree house her castle and batted off all intruders. She cut a powerful figure but she couldn't forget something that had been said by one of the other girls, 'She's not very nice, is 'er? 'Er needs to learn some manners.' Professor Howard-Jones explains that grudges have their genesis in the wiring of the brain because regions of the brain associated with making memory (the hippocampus) and regions associated with negative emotions (the amygdala) are right next to each other. This makes it quicker for an emotional event to activate our memory-making equipment, producing an emotional memory that's hard to shift; in other words, a grudge.

Writing this book has given us the opportunity to compare children *across* ages, not something we do in the series, and there's so much to learn from the comparison in these pivotal years of their lives. For example, when four-year-old Lola is asked to show a photo of her family to the group from the front of the classroom she looks intently at the photo in her hand, oblivious to fact that none of her (bored and yawning) classmates can see what she is looking at. By contrast, six-year-old Elvin holds his map of the London Underground up high above his head and asks, 'Can you all see it?' Elvin has learnt what Lola is still to grasp – that what is in his mind is different to what is in the minds of his friends; they are not always seeing what he is seeing.

But it was clear straight away that children do not achieve their developmental milestones at the same time. A year is a long time in the life of a young child and often we saw more difference between two four-year-olds than between a four and a five-year-old, or even a four and a six-year-old.

Luke: Do you want to come to my party? Sweetcorn will be there. Pizza will be there. Caramel . . . ?

The Secret Life of 4, 5 and 6 Year Olds never set out to be a parenting programme, but one of the heart-warming responses from parents has been that watching the show

and listening to experts unpicking the range of behaviour in the playground has made them feel less worried about their own child's behaviour. As a parent, seeing one's child misbehaving can be uncomfortable; at worst it can feel like an indictment of one's parenting skills. By offering a window onto the things the children got up to in a world with few adults – the tussles, the name-calling, the disagreements and arguments – the programme gave parents the chance to see that it really wasn't all that bad, and to sit back and enjoy what might have seemed negative behaviour in their own children.

But I hope the series also shines a light on how smart and competent children really are when they are left to their own devices. We were amazed to see how well they mastered challenges, expressed their emotions, made friends, dealt with disappointment and rejection, even making a good fist of winning and losing. One teacher told me that the series had changed the way she taught her class of five-year-olds. 'I've realized,' she said, 'that they're capable of far more than I thought they were. I ask more of them now and I leave them to resolve more of their own conflicts. I only step in when I need to.'

What do shepherds do at Christmas?
Luke: Did they make lasagne?

This book is intended as a celebration, companion and extension to the TV series. More than a hundred children have now passed through, and there is so much to admire in each and every one of them. Television is an ephemeral medium and it isn't often you get the chance to go back and take another look. It's been a great pleasure to be reminded how special it was to watch their interactions, how much we learnt from them, and how much they learnt from each other. If nothing else, I hope you'll agree that some of the things they said needed collecting together in one place.

The book takes the television series as a starting point, but it goes further by suggesting these children have some interesting lessons for us all in the way they approach life. This is not a self-help book, rather it's a chance to reflect on children's behaviour and how it changes and develops over time, which has always been a big part of the show.

It is structured around the key challenges that our four, five or six-year-olds have faced, and these are things

that we can all recognize as part of our lives too. Whether that's making friends, learning to be a good loser (and winner), or dealing with temptation and channelling our emotions.

Each chapter draws on examples of four, five *and* six-year-olds, and looks to the science of our brains for context and a better understanding. And, like the show, the chapters are full of the brilliant and hilarious things the children said and did.

Above all, this book celebrates the extraordinary children who have contributed to the programmes and given us such insight, pleasure and joy along the way. All of us who've had the privilege of working on the series have felt, at one time or another, that we were seeing our biggest or most painful emotions writ large, as expressed by one child or another.

These children take us down a path back to our early lives – a world we dimly remember but cannot always grasp. Their ability to evoke in us a forgotten past is at once very funny, tremendously powerful and immensely moving.

making friends

Every episode of *The Secret Life of 4, 5 and 6 Year Olds* begins with a group of children meeting each other for the very first time. We wanted a situation that was instantly recognizable and one that we could all relate to. Each child took those first tentative steps towards getting to know the other children all by themselves, and had to work out how to negotiate the minefield of social interaction on the way to making friends. Watching them over the course of the week they spent together, it was clear that, whether they were four, five or six, they made genuine and reciprocal friendships. And those friendships have given us some of the funniest, touching and best-loved moments of the show so far.

How many years are you and Alfie going to be friends?
Emily: Not years, forever. Forever.

We all know the feeling of being in an unfamiliar situation and meeting a group of people for the first time, whether it is the first day at a new school, a new job or going to an evening class. Some of us take new situations in our stride, find it easy to make small talk, picking up acquaintances and friends easily. But most of us have felt awkward at some time or another and have struggled with the conventions – how to break the ice, when to speak and when to listen, even how to say hello and goodbye. Kisses on both cheeks? Neither? But at some point those tentative, even awkward, exchanges transform into friendship.

What quickly becomes clear from watching the children is that there are no hard and fast rules of meeting, greeting and making friends. It is not a skill we are born with; no one teaches us how to do it and we make up the rules as we go along through trial and error. Sometimes we get it right, sometimes we misfire spectacularly. And yet the children do make friends, and really good friends too.

And this is important because so much of what we see happening is applicable throughout our lives. We all need

Do you think friends are important? Jadzia: Yes, because if you didn't have a friend you'll be lonely.

friends whatever age we are. Friends not only enhance the *quality* of our lives, sharing experiences, excitements, joys and sorrows, now we're told they also enhance the *quantity*, helping us to live longer, healthier lives. We are primates; we live in a social world and we are social beings. We instinctively watch what our fellow beings are up to and we make connections, we relate. It's what we're programmed to do.

Are we hardwired to make friends?

We are born with a brain that automatically 'reads' social signals – a tendency to look at eyes and faces, to listen to speech and to exchange signals with others – and this primes our brains to attend to the 'world of others'. These social exchanges help to shape our developing brain, encouraging an impressive range of social skills to emerge by four years old. These include the language and empathy we need to make friends.

Friendships help us in so many ways as individuals. They encourage us to think and to learn, and they also provide a stress-buffer – when facing a difficult situation, having a friend around can make it less likely we will experience stress, reducing our tendency to produce the stress hormone cortisol. In some challenging situations, young children can find it as helpful having a friend around as a parent – at least in terms of keeping their stress levels down.

What is friendship?
Alfie: I don't know. I never asked anybody yet. When I go back I'll ask Mamma.

What is friendship?

It feels like an odd question to ask and, like Alfie, you might feel it's not something you're equipped to answer. We all feel we know innately what friendship is, but as soon as we start to think about it we find it takes many different shapes in different contexts.

Watching the children as they begin to form friendships is pleasurable in its own right, but it's also fascinating to look at the different skills involved in making friends for the light it can shed on our own ability to make and sustain friendships. The children's relationships are every bit as complex as ours though they very often have their roots in a very simple act: that of sharing.

Christian: Sharing is how you make friends.

What happens when we share?

An important basis for any relationship is trust. Many friendships begin with sharing; it's an important sign of trust. When we think we are being trusted we experience an increase in levels of the 'anti-stress' hormone oxytocin and that encourages us to invest trust in others. In this way, through trust and our body's response to trust, sharing helps build an emotionally secure basis for collaboration and the beginning of a relationship.

Arguably, learning to share is the most important social skill we *ever* have to master because it forms the basis for pretty much every other social interaction for the rest of our lives. As we grow up we start by learning to share attention and our 'stuff' – toys, teddies, treats. Even conversation requires us to share opportunities to speak. We move on to sharing thoughts and feelings – 'I felt glad when you did that' (or 'sad' or 'mad'). And we go on to share *ideas*, the bits of us that make us who we are as unique individuals – our personal preferences, our taste in clothes, or music, or books, the kind of games we like to play, our likes and dislikes, our sense of humour. Once we can share all these things we have a firm basis for human interaction and for making friends.

Sharing is what scientists call a 'pro-social skill', in other words, a positive action that benefits other people. It is usually prompted by empathy, moral values and a sense of personal responsibility, rather than a desire for personal gain.

Jessica: I can stay friends with people.
Teacher: For a long time?
Jessica: Until I die.

Important as it is, it can also be hard work. We saw the perfect illustration of just how hard when four-year-old Skyla was given a bar of chocolate in front of her friends.

It was her last day at the play centre, and all the children were given a going-home present – Skyla's was a bar of chocolate. There were five pieces. Her four friends looked longingly at the chocolate in her hands. 'Sharing is caring, Skyla,' piped up one. Skyla wanted to

do the right thing, but she also desperately wanted to keep the chocolate all for herself. She tried out various strategies, from 'I'll eat it before it melts' to 'I don't think there's enough for everyone', and time stood still. It was agonizing to watch her try and delay the inevitable.

'Do I have to . . . ?'

Then, out of nowhere, a boy called Chaim, who had been watching through the window, saw his chance, dashed in and nicked one of her precious pieces of chocolate in a masterful snatch-and-grab. To be fair he *did* ask; he just didn't wait for the answer.

Instantly there was a common enemy, the spell was broken and the indecision was over. As a sobbing Skyla was comforted by her friends, she shared out the remaining chocolate with the girls and they played happily together for the rest of the afternoon. Of course she wasn't just sharing the chocolate, she was sharing the drama too – always a bonding experience among friends.

What makes this scene relatable is the way Skyla expresses so eloquently what we all feel sometimes. It's a natural instinct to hoard things for ourselves, but most of the time we suppress this instinct for the common good.

How do you make friends with people?

Jayda: Just say hello to them and say your names.

Chaim: Be nice.

Cuba: Say it like you're a nice person and then they'll be your friend.

Lola: I only have two friends. I'm trying to get some more so I get like fifty, one hundred, eight.

We saw this impulse to cement friendships by sharing when four-year-old Luke passed four-year-old Jessica a bead for the bracelet she was making, and then asked, 'Are you going to be my best friend now?' And having met up with old pal Skyla after six months only to be told that Skyla didn't remember her, Jessica felt this same urge to share a story as a way to rekindle their friendship.

Jessica: When I was a baby I got swine flu, and swine flu is when you get a bit too hot. I went at the doctors, I was nearly dead and my heart couldn't breathe.

Skyla: So you died?

Jessica: I didn't die but I nearly.

Skyla: So was your heart bleeding?

Jessica: No. Our hearts doesn't bleed, does it? Only our brain's got blood.

Piquing Skyla's interest in this way did the trick and they played together, more or less happily, for the rest of the week.

Why does it feel good to have a friend?

Using neuroimaging, scientists have been able to study the reward response in our brain that kicks in when we anticipate concrete rewards like money or chocolate. Friends can be a source of *social* reward such as praise and flattery. Now, however, scientists have noticed that these social rewards stimulate the same kind of response in our brains as the more concrete ones. In fact, this response occurs when we simply share attention with someone else in a game or social activity, encouraging us to get socially involved.

So how do strategies for making friends change and develop across the four, five and six-year-olds?

The four-year-olds

When the four-year-olds come into the room for the very first time, it's apparent straight away that they relate more to the teacher than to each other. They naturally seek out the attention of the adult in the room. We do see some heart-warming friendships developing but they are often short lived and fluid, with the children moving in and out of them with relative ease. And their four-year-old strategies are pretty direct: 'Play with me', 'Be my friend', 'Do this', 'Do that'. Sometimes it works; sometimes it's off-putting.

One particularly moving example was the friendship between Tyler and Theo, and it struck a chord with everyone who saw it.

Tyler's mum put him up for the programme because she wanted a glimpse of how he got on with other children when she wasn't around. She was concerned that he had a way of playing that was very solitary, even when his little sister was around: 'His attention is fantastic but it's only on what he wants. I don't think Tyler feels the pressure of being liked. He's in his own bubble. And he loves it. He doesn't feel any need to make friends.'

Only child Theo attends a Steiner school. A boy with a vivid imagination, he came to us intent on finding a friend. He was immediately drawn to classmate Tyler and

one day, early on, Theo sat down where Tyler was playing to tell him about his dream.

Tyler, meanwhile, carried on driving his two red buses, making quite loud bus noises as they went on their way. Theo had to comfort himself for his scary dream and he didn't understand why Tyler didn't want to play with him.

But Theo didn't give up. Undeterred and with great ingenuity, Theo realized that a Hula Hoop made the perfect friend-catcher. He lay in wait and then lassoed his friend, saying simply:

> Theo: I had a bad dream last night, with a wolf going to side to side in our house and he's come upstairs and got me! That was a bad dream. I don't like it.

> Theo: Why won't my friend play with me? I was talking to him and he doesn't listen to me. He just loves his buses.

> Theo: Get that boy! I need him.

Somewhere in this exchange Tyler woke up to the fact that Theo wanted to play with him and a smile crept across his face. He began to enjoy the game and didn't even mind being brought crashing to the ground. Theo's direct approach paid off. Tyler reciprocated and they spent the rest of the week playing together.

The skill of noticing cues for friendship and engaging with them isn't automatic – it happens at different ages for different children. And we can still get it wrong as an adult. As one viewer said, 'I'm going to get myself one of those friend-catcher hoops . . .'

What's in a smile?

Our social behaviour is strongly influenced by how we respond to the emotional signals that others send out. If someone smiles, for example, it can make it more likely we will approach them. Scientists have found that the impact of another's smile on our brain can even help predict our future. When researchers measured how the brains of adults responded to the smiles of those they'd already met, they found they could make a reasonable forecast of friendship patterns some months later.

If you watch much younger children playing, you can chart their social interaction developing as they acquire new skills: they start off playing by themselves but quite soon they become interested in other people's play, maybe throwing in the odd question or comment as a way of engaging with it. Soon after, they start playing alongside a playmate, in parallel with someone else. Sometimes you hear two and three-year-olds mimicking each other's play even though they seem to be playing separate games. By four years old, most children are beginning to develop the skills to play together. Scientists refer to this as 'co-operative play' where typically there is a common goal and activities are shared out. We saw countless, beautiful examples of co-operative play: four-year-olds like Theo and Tyler watering the allotment together, sharing a watering can and looking for strawberries, or four-year-olds picking up cues in imaginary games, whether it's going shopping, cooking a meal, taking your kitten for a walk in the park, or just comparing bottoms:

Tia: I am a princess who has a beautiful dress.

Theo: I'm a boy that shakes my bottom.

Ivar: Whoa, stop that, stinking bottom.

Tia: Here's my bottom if you'd like to see it.

Many a friendship was formed and cemented through this new kind of play.

The five-year-olds

In contrast we saw friendships becoming deeper and more complex among our five-year-olds, with small slights and rejections being remembered and informing how friendships and enmities played out over the week. Take Ruth, for example, who was never forgiven for winning a medal in a dance contest that Jaja felt was rightfully hers, or Oscar, who bore a grudge over several days when his best mate Oliver dumped him for new girl, Naomi.

And we began to see instances of humour sustaining friendships across the week; George and Lily, for example, who found the same things funny, like the sight of George struggling to carry a deckchair across to come and sit next to her:

George: It's kicking my booty.
Lily: What's a booty?

In fact they laughed whenever they were together and teased each other like old friends – Lily made fun of his middle name, Fernando, and George got his own back in a portrait painting task: 'I'm going to do you bald.'

At five years old, after one year of school, we saw children becoming aware of their relationship to the group as a whole and looking for friends with whom they shared interests.

Alfie: I love you.
Emily: I missed you so much.

And among our five-year-olds it didn't get better than best friends Emily and Alfie. Emily lives with her mum and grandma and, according to them, she's one of a kind. Emily told us she wanted to be a 'jelly maker, a pencil sharpener or a toy maker' when she grew up. Her mum says she has a lot of empathy for other people and is wise beyond her years. She wears glasses to keep control of what she calls her 'wonky eye' and, as Grandma Brenda says, 'She faults herself because she has to wear glasses,' but adds that she's quite unique and, 'She just instantly makes friends with people.'

Which is what happened with Alfie, as they immediately found shared interests and common ground. Alfie doesn't wear glasses but he does have hearing aids, and when a dinosaur mask got tangled up in them Emily asked why, in that refreshingly straightforward way that children have, and he explained they help him hear properly. 'I can hear fine,' Emily replied, 'it's just my eye. Like your hearing aids, I have glasses, they help me see.'

Whether it was their glasses and hearing aids, a love of singing nonsense words or playing Rolling Disease, a game which involved rolling over and over and over in the grass until you swoon with dizziness and burst out laughing, it was a meeting of minds. Alfie is bright and articulate, an expert on trains, Roald Dahl, nutrition and pretty much anything he turns his attention to, but he sometimes struggles with friends, as his mum told us: 'Making friends

has always been difficult for Alfie. Play with other children is usually very much governed by his rules, but when he plays with Emily it is a very organic natural process with no power struggles – just an equal understanding of whatever it is they are doing. Emily completely understood Alfie from day one. They were inseparable that week they met and missed each other terribly in the weeks that followed.'

Emily: What's another way you can get the Rolling Disease?
Alfie: Oh, I know, touching the grass.
Emily: Okay, pick pick pick, yay. Cowabunga. This is so much fun.

It seemed to us that five-year-olds enjoyed the ability to form real and sustained friendships while still being able to dip in and out of fantasies and the real world all around them.

Cuba: Vegan means I don't eat any meat or cow's milk or anything, I just eat oranges and spinach and stuff like that.

Chaim: You obviously can have at least one piece of chocolate.

Kash: What's your name?

Chaim: Chaim.

Kash: Keean?

Chaim: No, Chaim.

Kash: Kyam?

Chaim: No, Chaim.

Kash: Hyam.

Chaim: Chaim!

Kash: (Laughs, giving up)

The six-year-olds

By six years old we saw a whole different approach; where the four-year-olds were direct and focused on the grown-ups, the six-year-olds were immediately more interested in each other, and we saw them respond to both overt cues and subtle clues as they were introduced. And with their greatly increased language skills and empathy they began to show real curiosity, asking each other lots of questions, and to play around with their own identity in playful, teasing ways:

Elvin: When I was born I wasn't this colour actually I was just white. And then my skin grew black and black and black.

Taye: All of my family's skin colour is black.

Austyn: I think you mean brown, not black.

Taye: Yeah, browny. Yeah. A bit browny.

They were constantly comparing, and working out where they stood in relation to the group, being competitive with each other about everything, and assessing the natural hierarchy that began to establish itself from the moment they met:

> Kash: Austyn, d'you wanna be my friend?

> Austyn: Uh-huh.

> Boy 1: My mum is fifty.

> Boy 2: My mum is fifty-nine.

> Kash: My mum is older than all of your mums.

> Kash: D'you wanna be his as well? I'm the boss of the gang, and this is Caspar. I'm the boss of the gang.

> Why do you like to be friends with Beatrice?

> Elvin: Because she helps people.

> What makes Elvin a good friend do you think, Beatrice?

> Beatrice: Good games.

Six-year-olds like Beatrice and Elvin clearly had a real rapport, and their friendship was based on shared interests, a shared perspective and shared jokes. Just like five-year-olds George and Lily, six-year-olds Elvin and Beatrice found the same things funny, including wordplay:

Elvin: Welcome on board this Southeastern service to Nunhead.

Beatrice: Nun-head?

Elvin: (Laughing) Nun. Head.

Beatrice: (Laughing) Nunhead!

Elvin: That's actually a real station in London.

The six-year-olds were aware of adult mechanisms for friendship and their sense of time was becoming more sophisticated – they realized friendships could exist beyond the present moment.

Elvin: Er, Beatrice, can I tell you something? This morning when I was coming here, yeah, I was trying to send you a text message, Beatrice. I said 'Good morning Beatrice, how are you?' And I couldn't be . . . because . . .

Beatrice: You didn't know my phone number? Shall I ask my mum tonight, erm, to tell you, erm, my mum's phone number?

Elvin: Okay. You might – you might want to connect your iPad to my phone because then I – I'll be able to send you a text message.

But of course making friends isn't easy

The fact is that it takes courage and a fairly complex set of social skills to make friends. In *Secret Life* we see many heartbreaking examples of the four-year-olds making repeated unsuccessful bids for friendship; a child may be very sociable, very affable, but not always very assertive in their attempts. It's every parent's nightmare – seeing your child alone in the playground with no one to play with. But simply asking someone to play with you isn't always enough – you have to have something to offer, like a toy or a good idea – and taking a risk with a potential new friend can be hard without some degree of assertiveness.

Intriguingly, Professor Howard-Jones tells us that being sociable and being assertive are quite distinct types of behaviour involving different circuits in our brain, so it is possible to have one without the other – to be very sociable but not very good at asserting yourself. We saw this with Taysia, who took some time to find a friend in spite of repeated attempts.

Is it ever difficult to make friends?

Taysia: Sometimes if they keep running around.

And what happens then?

Taysia: You go run and chase after them.

Two's company

No sooner were friendships forged than fallings out followed, and never more so than when a twosome became a threesome. In friendship three really does seem to be a crowd.

Research suggests that from as young as a few months old, girls respond more to photographs of pairs of people, whereas boys respond more to photographs of groups. This may be the reason that the girls in *Secret Life* tended to seek out a tight 'best friend' whereas the boys seemed to be more at ease in larger groups. Time and again we saw instances of girl meets girl, new girl comes to join in the game, new girl pushes out first girl. Cue rejection and heartbreak.

It was agonizing to watch.

Our scientists, however, were quick to point out that this is happening in playgrounds all over the country and it may have real purpose for the children in a developmental sense. This kind of tussling over friendships, marginalizing one member and forming in-groups and out-groups is simply the children's way of exploring the concept of friendship and the strong emotions it evokes.

As psychologist Dr Sam Wass commented, 'If you give a child a new abstract concept to play with, such as the concept of a friendship, the natural instinct of a child is to want to prod and explore what that idea is all about. They tug it around a bit, see if they can break it, and by doing this they learn more about what the concept of friendship means.'

The girls use role play to test out what is acceptable and what isn't, to learn that their actions have reactions and to establish the rules of friendship. The rejection is palpable, painful and real, but it is also experienced

Princess A: Shall we play princesses but nice princesses without her?

Princess B: No, we need to try and make her upset.

Princess A: Super girls! (They high five)

Princess B: Let's go make her angry.

within the boundaries of the game and this makes it relatively safe to experiment with. As one dad puts it, 'Oh yes, she falls out with her friends all the time. I think she enjoys the drama.'

There are fewer examples among the boys, but there was one trio in which three was definitely a crowd. Five-year-olds Oliver and Oscar bonded as soon as they first met over hairstyles, dancing and football, and they became best buddies. When new girl, Naomi, arrives the following week and decides that Oliver is boyfriend material, Oscar is left in the lurch. And in the ultimate rebuff, during a game of Mums and Dads, Oscar is told to play the child:

As it turns out, the real romance at the heart of this trio is between the two boys, and once they mend their friendship Naomi can once again be included in their play.

We saw this kind of falling out time and again – children could be best friends in the morning, enemies in the afternoon, and it would all be resolved by teatime. It was dizzying, but the beauty of friendship at this age is that, however keenly the slings and arrows are felt, these children live in the moment and enmities are quickly forgotten. They are able to move on much more freely than we do as adults.

Oscar: Hey, I don't want to be the kid.

Oliver: Well you can be the teenager then.

Oscar: Okay, but no smooching.

Oscar: We had a little argument and it wasn't good but then we sorted it all out.

Tell me about you guys being best friends.

Oscar: It's just easy in life if we're best friends.

arguments

Caitlyn: You're not coming to my birthday.

George: The sun's made out of lava.

Kash: I don't even wanna come, because where d'you go for your birthday?

Alfie: No, the sun's not made out of lava, it's made out of gas, you blimmin' bummox.

Caitlyn: Build-A-Bear Workshop where you can make your own teddy bear.

George: No, it's made out of lava.

Kash: Well I'm going to a bigger place.

Alfie: I looked in books and it said it was made out of gas you big lummox.

George: They're wrong, it's made out of lava.

Caitlyn: I'm having two birthday parties.

Alfie: No, gas.

Kash: Well I'm gonna have three parties . . .

George: Lava.

Caitlyn: Now you're just being more rude.

Alfie: Gas.

George: Lava.

Kash: How am I being rude? Is that being rude, Caspar? I, I'm having even more birthdays, I'm having three, is that being rude?

Alfie: My dear old fish, go and boil your head.

The lasting impact of friends

Theo and Tyler

In a touching postscript to the story of Theo and Tyler and the friend-catcher, Tyler's mum, Nikita, wrote us a letter after Tyler had started in Reception, saying, 'He still talks about what a fantastic time he had, and it made such a difference to his social skills. Tyler is more sociable with children at big school and he is more open to joining in now, and I attribute this to Theo breaking down that barrier within him. Tyler still mentions Theo all the time. As for Theo, that kid will go far in life with his resilience and perseverance to see rejection as an opportunity. He encouraged my son in ways no one else has been able to.' Theo and Tyler still FaceTime each other.

Emily and Alfie

According to Alfie's mum, two years on he still refers to Emily as his 'true love', and Emily recently wrote a note to him telling him that he is the love of her life too. They are still in regular contact and they're adamant they will marry as adults. Alfie recently wrote Emily a letter which read, 'To the person I will never stop loving. Hearts are pink, very very hot stars are blue, but nothing is as beautiful and intelligent as you.'

Why does it feel so good to see an old friend?

Our past emotional experience with a particular person can have long-lasting effects on how the memory of their face is stored in our brain. When we see that person again, this close intertwining of past emotions with our memory of their face can trigger an automatic emotional response. So, when we spot an old friend (or foe), our feelings can start surfacing before we even know what's happening.

Do we ever stop being able to make friends?

We show a tendency towards social behaviour from the first year of life, but that's only the first step. The challenge of making friends and learning about friendship is one that continues throughout our lives. The good news is that our brains retain enough lifelong plasticity to enable us to do this, and our social behaviour continues to shape our brains until our dying day. In fact, the size of some parts of our adult brains – such as those involved with remembering social information – can be predicted by the number of friends we have on social network sites like Facebook. We never lose our ability to make friends, or the opportunity to improve it!

A guide to . . .

Ask questions

Alfie: I live in Somerset. Where do you live?

George: What part of Africa do you live in? Cos I went there before.

Ellie: Shall I show you how to do the splits?

Show someone something – your seashells, your map of the London Underground, your special foot, your bottom . . .

Lola: Look, there it is. That's the little nubbie. That's what's special about me.

Pay someone a compliment

Ruth: George, that's a nice name.

Calla: You are an amazing singer!

Caitlyn: My hairstyle is getting badder and badder.

Poppy: It's fabulous.

making friends

Don't command someone to be your friend

Ellie: Jude! That's not funny, Jude. Behave, behave!

Jude: You can't tell me, you're not the boss of here . . .

Don't make personal comments

George: Look at your face. Look, you've got a chicken nugget face.

Alfie: I need someone to play cheetahs with or I won't ever allow you to be here again.

Jadzia: Come on. Chop chop, girl. Chop chop.

Tia: I'm coming now, bossy.

Jadzia: I'm not bossy.

Tia: You are.

little grown-ups

George: Hello. This is the President of the USA talking. A fire?! I'll be there right away, after I make myself a cake. Bye bye.

One of the children's favourite places in the *Secret Life* play centre is the 'Home Corner', where they can lay the table, cook a meal, make the beds and dress up. They can even go to the toilet and forget to flush it. It's a magical adult world in miniature where children can recreate scenes they've encountered in their everyday life with their newly acquired friends.

In a bid to understand the world around them the children borrow the patterns and language of grown-ups and play around with it, trying out different roles and different turns of phrase for size. This is often where some of the funniest moments in the show have come from, but it also tells us something about how we all learn through imitation, then apply this in our own relationships. This means that the language of their play is peppered with phrases they have heard in the adult world:

We're going to make a chilli, darling.

I'm on the computer, kids.

Who left the toilet poo-ey? Sorry Dad!

Tell your mum that I'll be there in a minute . . . Hello? Oh, for God's sake. For God's sake, I'm gonna have to text her.

We're playing Mums and Dads – oh no, I forgot the baby.

We're not gonna smooch yet, because we're not old enough. We're gonna smooch when we're about thirteen or whatever.

Why do children imitate what they see and hear?

One of the first ways that children discover learning is observational learning – or 'learning by watching'. By two years old a child can imitate someone they don't even know, without speech or any other sign of interaction taking place.

Children have a natural tendency to imitate the things they see adults doing, and to combine these things into new and imaginative scenarios. To keep the fantasy going, they have to keep returning to the question of what might happen next. This causes them to question, argue and justify their ideas about the world to each other. It also encourages them to encounter new ideas and new ways of looking at things. In this way, what starts as simple imitation can often become a rich opportunity for learning through play.

How does children's relationship to the adult world change as they get older?

At four years old we are squarely in the world of the imagination, and children can pluck ideas from the adult world freely and share them collaboratively; no one questions when a boat is conjured out of thin air, a piece of cloth passes as a wedding dress or a boy becomes a pet crocodile for a bride and groom. That said, four-year-old Tia wanted to keep things age-appropriate:

Taylor: Rock stars, rock stars, rock stars.

Tia: No, no, no, we're not rock stars, we're just children, okay? So sit down and don't talk!

Taylor: You're being rude to me.

Tia: Alright, you can talk, but just don't say we're rock stars, okay.

A guide to . . .

What age do you become a grown-up?

Lewis: When you're like big, big, big, big, big, big.

Ellie-Mae: This is hard. Fifty-two or something.

What does it mean to be a grown-up?

Ellie: Washing up, cooking dinner. (Burps) Playing with people. Watch TV.

If you were king for one day what would you do?

Fabian: I will fly because I want to be a butterfly.

Lily: I like looking in the mirror, do you know? Because I like seeing when I'm gorgeous – I do. I always do selfies.

What do princesses do?

Jaja: Princess Jaja is me. But I don't want to be a princess, I want to be a queen.

Jaja: Don't fart!

growing up

What do you want to be when you grow up?

Charlotte:
Hairdresser and a doctor.

Christian:
A policeman.

Jack:
Save the planet.

Layton: I've got a lion mane and when I grow up I'll have a big beard and if I be very special lion whiskers might grow out of my freckles.

Alfie: Eventually I want to go in a rocket and blast off into space. I could build myself one of just the right kind.

Caitlyn: I want to be a nurse cos I really like animals.

Elouisa: Pop star. Yeah, yeah, yeah, a pop star.

Ellie: I wanna be a vet on Monday, Tuesday, Wednesday, Thursday, Friday and I wanna be the queen on Saturday and Sunday.

Skyla: I don't want to grow up!

The Secret Life of 4, 5 and 6 Year Olds

By age five the children's games began to teeter between the world of make-believe and the real world. Sometimes they cross over and become too real, and at this point the children have to check whether they're playing by the same rules.

Take this game of Doctors and Nurses in which Dr Ellie-Mae had some bad news to break to patient Ellie:

Ellie-Mae had experience of hospitals and illness first hand and the game took on shades of her reality that were challenging for Ellie to play along with. But in general, children's fantasy play proved a safe space in which to explore real-life situations and events, conversations overheard or real emotions being processed. And as our five-year-olds began to draw more and more on their knowledge of the real world, so the games became more revealing, and the line between what was real and what was fantasy became more blurred.

By six years old, after another year of school, the children were showing even more interest in what's real and what's not:

Ellie-Mae: You go up to heaven, yeah? Well I know you'll go to heaven or hell. Hell's when you've been bad. When you've been good you go to heaven. And heaven is a good . . .

Ellie: (Interrupting) I . . . I am a little child, did you know?

Caitlyn: Why did you want to leave the clubhouse?

Poppy: I wanted it to be a game.

Caitlyn: But a club isn't a game. A club is a real thing.

Poppy: That's why I didn't want to be joining in.

Caitlyn: We're just too old to play those games that aren't real. We're too old to play them.

Elvin: Hello, we're back on *Sky News*. There was an attack on the French train to Paris. They got the knife and got the guard and stabbed them—

Beatrice: And even killed the conductor. Woo . . . sad news, isn't it?

In another playtime, international terrorism became the theme of the game as the six-year-olds mimicked a news broadcast and reported on, among other things, a terrorist attack on a train:

Elvin: Next, a plane attack in Surrey on the S21. I've got to hand over to Taye at the S21 that's been closed off.

Taye: So let's just watch that plan for a sec.

Beatrice: Kash, get out of the way, you'll be filmed. We're on set now.

It's a salutary reminder that children absorb information like sponges. Talking to them about these things is important so that they can understand the significance of given events and the value that adults attach to them. If there's one general piece of wisdom that's come out of the show, it's that children are much more capable of dealing with stuff than we tend to think.

It must be love

Among the sweetest, funniest and most touching strands of play are the romances that get acted out in front of us. We couldn't have a book about the children in *Secret Life* without including their thoughts on love and romance; at times the children have moved us to tears and at other times they have kept us on the edge of our seats with a will-they, won't-they cliff-hanger – to kiss or not to kiss. It is a common idea among four, five and six-year-olds that a kiss carries considerable weight:

What does being married mean?
Orlagh: You live together.
Layton: And kiss together. (Laughing)
And cuddle together.

The language may be borrowed from fairy tales, films and TV, but we were repeatedly struck by the strength of affection between these children, and the charm of their innocent displays of grown-up emotions:

Layton: My darling, it's church time! Quick, my darling! Our boat is leaving to our wedding.

Layton lives in Essex, with his mum and dad. According to them he's a 'ladies' man' and we met him spraying some strawberry aftershave on his socks to 'make them smell gooder'. Orlagh introduced herself to the group by pointing out that she had a cold sore. They both love playing imaginative games and, at four years old, Layton and Orlagh are immersed in the language of make-believe – 'This is like Rapunzel's hair,' Layton says admiringly to one of his toys.

Layton arrived with the express intention of finding a girlfriend and seeing Orlagh dressed as a witch he starts up a game. As well as fragrant socks, Layton thinks girls are 'gooder' too and Orlagh appreciates this, 'He's like a girl, actually, cos he's nice and not rough.' And before long they're snuggling down for the night in a beautiful piece of collaborative play.

Of course, Layton isn't letting on that he actually made a bid for someone else the week before, another four-year-old called Amelia-Rose. Sadly for Layton, when he asked if Amelia-Rose would like to marry him, she said, 'I've already got someone to marry, someone called Daniel':

Layton: Why are you marrying Daniel instead of me?

Amelia-Rose: Because I just kissed him.

Layton: On the lips?

Amelia-Rose: Yeah. And you can't go kissing too many mans.

But it turns out it was worth the wait for Orlagh and Layton, and true love is announced, in time-honoured fashion, via a joke:

Orlagh: Knock knock.

Layton: Who's there.

Orlagh: Layton.

Layton: Layton who?

Orlagh: Layton-loved-by-Orlagh.

Layton beams like the cat who's got the cream. With the four-year-olds we would often see this glorious lack of self-consciousness, with detail after detail plucked from stories, TV and film, magpie-like and with a total suspension of disbelief. In Layton and Orlagh's case they managed to engage the whole group in their game:

Layton: Now, everyone! Invite to our wedding! So, it's quarter past eight now, so we need to get married, right now. Quarter past eight now. Got to get going . . . We need to marry now. Just quick. We'll marry now. Just quick.

There's just one obstacle:

Layton: Wait . . . ! Remember you've got a coleslaw. Don't kiss tonight because you've got a coleslaw, remember? Good. Shall we do one cuddle?

Orlagh: No. Even if you do cuddles you get coleslaws.

At four years old, Layton knows that he and Orlagh have to kiss to get married and that the knot won't be sealed until they do. The charm lies in the lack of embarrassment. Let's compare this for a moment with our six-year-olds and see how the significance of a kiss has changed for the older children.

Elouisa: Kash! Kash, I actually have fallen in love with you.

Six-year-olds Kash and Elouisa earmark each other from the first time they meet. They also know that a kiss carries weight and can signify a girlfriend–boyfriend situation. And, by six, an element of secrecy – both the thrill and the potential embarrassment – has crept in. First, the rules of the game are of paramount importance:

Charlie O: I know the kissing rules.

Kash: What?

Charlie O: If you put lipstick on someone, and if you kiss someone with lipstick on . . .

Kash: . . . they'll know.

Second, it must be done out of the overseeing eye of the teacher . . . and even of the cameras:

Elouisa: I have to make sure they stay still and then I have to kiss them all, okay? Shall we call this trap Operation Kiss?

And third, the status bestowed by a kiss – the status of boyfriend/girlfriend *within the group* – has become all-important. With the six-year-olds the group comes first, and one's standing within the group takes precedence over one's own desires. It is peer pressure in action. Kash adores the attentions of Elouisa – his cool swagger doesn't fool us for a minute:

> Elouisa: Can we get married?

> Kash: Fine, I'll just do it then. I'll just do it, I don't care, I'll just do it. I do wanna get married.

> Elouisa: Then I'll just tell my boyfriend – other boyfriend.

Elouisa and Kash embark on a romantic roller-coaster; it is an exciting but unstable friendship which starts with Kiss Chase, then swiftly moves through proposal, marriage and bust up, all in a week. A valuable learning experience for them both as they try out their ideas around love in a safe environment:

What is love?
Elouisa: Love. Love is love, love . . . and it is love, is love, this is gonna carry on for a – a long while.

Bridging this gap between our four-year-olds, with their touching lack of social awkwardness, and our six-year-olds, already self-conscious in front of their peers, is one of the most touching romances we have seen in *Secret Life* – that of Arthur and Sienna.

Arthur: I think we should be wedding people.

Never has a golden tea cosy been put to such good use as in this task in which the children were asked to dress their partner in a competition for the Best-Dressed Couple. Initially Sienna just cared about her own outfit, but when she was reminded that she must address Arthur's outfit too she tried to get to grips with the tea cosy, 'I'll hold your hat. It's back to front.' Asked to present their team to the rest of the group, Arthur hesitated at first: 'She's, erm, a wedding girl. She has a pair of sunglasses.' And Sienna ran with this, 'He's a wedding boy.'

Already as good as betrothed, Sienna and Arthur were highly aware of the importance of a kiss, just like the four-year-olds, and as with the six-year-olds there was an added layer of furtiveness.

Sienna: We need to do a – a kiss on the lips to get married now.

Arthur: She's not looking.

Sienna: Just get down here. And then they can't see us. Now we can get married.

A guide to . . .

Where do babies come from?

> Amelia-Rose: Tummies.

And how do they get into the tummy?

> Amelia-Rose: The dad puts them in, by love.

> Sienna: They come from the stork. The stork brings them when they're at hospital.

How do babies get out of their mummy's tummies?

> Tia: Erm, well . . . the doctors pull it out of the nunny.

How many babies would you like to have?

> Enzo: Don't ask us!

> Charlie O: Sometimes you can have three or four or five or six. Gonna choose . . . One's gonna be Baby Anna and one's gonna be Baby Freddie and one's gonna be Baby Kevin.

babies

Ellie: No. Uh-uh. I really want a baby though.

Do you think it's fun to be a grown-up?

Elvin: Guys, you don't even know the secret about love.

Jayda: What is it?

Elvin: If you don't like your mum, yeah, being rude to you, when you get older you get to go with someone else and you can visit your mum but you will be living somewhere else. That's the secret about love.

As well as a hint of reluctance on Arthur's part:

Arthur: Okay, pretend we already did the kiss.

Sienna: We ain't even had our kiss yet.

Sienna: We haven't even got married yet.

Arthur: I'll come back later when I'm finished.

Arthur: Yeah. Got to go to work though.

Sienna: Will you buy me a ring while you're out? Just buy me a ring.

Later Sienna reminds Arthur that the knot isn't yet tied:

Sienna: Arthur, we never had our wedding. We never got our kiss at the wedding. Why didn't you do it?

Arthur: I don't know. Cos you didn't say you wanted to do it.

Sienna: I kept telling you.

But through this exchange a real friendship is cemented, and back in the classroom there is nowhere else to sit but next to each other, holding hands.

Jude: Are you gonna be in love with me?

Love, love me do

Five-year-olds Jude and Ellie were some of our most intriguing 'little grown-ups'. Unlike Sienna and Arthur, whose 'wedding' remained strictly rooted in fantasy, when Ellie and Jude met it was as if they recognized in one another a playful ability to adopt the imagery and rhetoric of adult love and romance, giving us the funniest of our *Secret Life* couplings.

When Jude came to play he was the first into the room and he immediately took charge asking teacher, Simon, if his real name was Simon Cowell. As other children came in he didn't hesitate to describe himself as 'possibly the most interesting person in the room'.

When he was just two-and-a-half years old Jude showed a shape to his mum and asked, 'Is this a parallelogram?' and his mum said, 'I don't know, Jude, I'm gonna have to Google it.' This has been her response ever since: 'I don't know, Jude, I'll have to Google it.' As an only child he and his mum do everything together and she says he is like a mini-teenager, 'He's always saying he can't wait to be an adult.'

Next came Ellie. She sat down right next to him and offered to show him how to do the splits. 'I can do the splits,' he says. Unfortunately Jude's trousers were a bit too tight. But there was chemistry.

What do you like about Jude?
Ellie: His hair is so fluffy. I love fluffy hair. Mmmm (nuzzles Jude's hair). It's all snuggly like a pillow.

The first thing they did together was paint each other's portrait. In conversation, Ellie mentioned she was going to be a queen when she was older, 'And then you're gonna be a king cos I'm gonna marry you actually.'

Ellie lives in Essex with her mum and dad. Ellie uses the language of betrothals, kings and queens, but Jude immediately ups the ante, asking, 'Are you gonna be in love with me?'

Already at this age there's a status attached to having a girlfriend or a boyfriend, and Jude didn't waste the opportunity of announcing it, calling across the playground, 'Girlfriend! Girlfriend! Girlfriend!' To which Ellie answered dutifully, and somewhat out of character, 'Yeah, I'm coming, my boyfriend.'

Here's how negotiations unfolded from there:

> Jude: Are you gonna be in love with me?

> Ellie: Yes.

> Jude: I'm gonna be in love with you.

> Ellie: Oh thanks.

> Jude: Shall we kiss yet?

> Ellie: No. Not yet, when we only get married and we have a baby.

> Jude: Yeah that's the only time we're gonna kiss.

> Ellie: Yep, I know that for a fact. My mum told me you can't kiss when you're a child.

All in all, Jude and Ellie spent two weeks together and their 'relationship' burnt bright and faded fast. When Jude fell short in a game involving looking after babies that actually cry, Ellie decided it was time for a change: 'He's really nice but I just don't wanna marry him.' And in a brutal public declaration she told Jude she had fallen for someone else, at lunchtime. Not only was he unceremoniously dumped, his replacement was sitting right next to him.

But as watching psychologist Dr Wass points out, if there's one thing we know about Jude it's that if he gets knocked down, he gets right back up again. And indeed no sooner had Ellie dumped Jude than we found out that Jude had already lined up a replacement. Pushing another girl, Ellie-Mae, on the roundabout he reminded her, 'You said you were gonna be my other girlfriend . . . D'you like me kissing you?'

She did. And, with this, Jude bounced back.

Do you know what romance is?
Jude: Romantic means like sweet and kind and beautiful.
Ellie: Does it mean excellent?

Watching children at this age as an adult can be instructive. As one of our junior colleagues remarked, the things that make someone good at relationships at this age will probably stand them in good stead on a date at any point in their life. Ask questions, share something about yourself, give compliments where appropriate and talk about how you feel and you probably won't go far wrong!

But is it real?

Kissing and romantic behaviours are very common among young children. Mostly these crop up as they explore the ideas around love and romance they've heard about from their family and friends, seen on the TV or discovered through other media. Some research suggests it may be the 'real thing' and that children can experience passionate love for another by around three or four years old. It certainly does seem that very young children are as likely to admit to being in love as adolescents, with a notable dip in love talk around ages eight to twelve. However, whether romantic concepts such as 'boyfriend' and 'girlfriend' mean the same to a four-year-old as a fourteen-year-old is a question scientists are still struggling to answer!

A guide to . . .

Avoid complicated situations at all costs

Lily: Who d'you wanna marry?

Alfie: Erm, you.

Lily: Me. Good answer. Who d'you wanna kiss?

Alfie: You.

Lily: Me. Do you not fancy Emily anymore?

Alfie: Not really.

Lily: What d'you wanna do with Emily? Just bin 'er? Do you want to bin 'er?

Teacher: (Shouts) Lunchtime!

Ask your mum's permission

Tia: Mum . . . I met a superhero and he's really nice. I really want to marry him, please Mum.

romance

Jessica: The wall can be my boyfriend. Sometimes at school I kiss the wall.

Improvise

Know where your heart lies
Do you want to get married?

Emmanuel: No, I just wanna stay with my mum, and dad.

Keep it simple
What is love?

Arthur: So if you love someone it means that you really like someone.

Don't put up with any weirdness

Tia: My mum doesn't like strangers. So adigos. Adigos, Joe.

Joe: Maybe I can be your pet crocodile?

Tia: Erm . . . Excuse me, we do not need a pet crocodile here, do we?

Don't suffer fools

Jessica: (On phone) Stop ringing me, Richard, you're not the dad. Okay, I don't love you anymore, I hate you now. Bye. See you later.

language and the
art of persuasion

Layton: Knock, knock.
Orlagh: Who's there?
Layton: Europe.
Orlagh: Europe who?
Layton: Hey, you just called me a great big poo!

One of the best jokes you'll ever hear, delivered exquisitely on *Secret Life* by four-year-old Layton. Proof, if we needed it, that four-year-olds have a great love of words and the things you can do with them.

'Why do you love words?' we asked another four-year-old, Enzo. 'Because they give me a lot of information,' he replied. His latest was 'trynamator'. 'That's a big word,' he said, 'it's three words connected together.'

And for use of vocabulary, what about two of our six-year-olds playing a game of skating in the playground, alighting effortlessly on the very words to describe it: 'Push, push, glide . . . push, push, glide . . .'

It's estimated that at three years old an average child (if such a thing exists) has a vocabulary of about 1,000 words. By age four that same child's vocabulary has expanded almost three times to 2,500–3,000 words, and it will almost double again before they turn five. The average four-year-old learns between four and six new words a day. At age five this goes up to between six and nine new words every day, taking their vocabulary up to 5,000 words by the end of the year. That's a five-fold increase in three years. No wonder developmental psychologists talk about an 'explosion' in language skills and acquisition.

The joy of children acquiring language is that we suddenly have this new way of understanding them, as they begin to describe their thoughts and feelings and how they see the world around them. It's what makes four, five and six-year-olds so fascinating to observe.

And four-year-olds tell it like it is: when four-year-old Tia is asked if she's ever seen Father Christmas she replies that, yes she has, but only when she was a 'short girl' and it couldn't be more accurate; when Joe is asked how he feels today and he says, 'Today, I'm a swordfish,' he means it; when Jayda's asked who visited baby Jesus in the stable she sifts through the information in her head and alights on, 'Sheeps. The Three Wise Men. And a penguin.'

And when Alfie is asked how his journey was, he says, with perfect recall:

South Bermondsey, Queen's Road Peckham, Peckham Rye, East Dulwich, North Dulwich, Tulse Hill, West Norwood, Gypsy Hill, Crystal Palace and Beckenham Junction.

Why does language take off when it does?

What gets the vocabulary spurt going at around eighteen months is still the subject of argument among scientists. Some believe that a child's sudden improvement in their ability to speak words accurately and meaningfully causes their language to accelerate rapidly. However, others believe development of language in the child's brain is more of a gradual and continuous process. It may simply be that learning words gives an infant the power to communicate and learn more words, and that it is this 'more begets more' effect that causes language to really take off.

Lola: I've got a really funny one. Three monkeys in a bath. The first monkey said, 'Ooh ooh aah aah,' and the other one said, 'Well put some cold in then.'

Kash: Do you wanna have a nice convo?

Austyn: What?

Evie-Rae: Why did the cow cross the road?

Kash: Do you know what 'convo' means?

Why did the cow cross the road?

Austyn: No.

Evie-Rae: Cos it wanted to go to the mooooooooooo-vies.

Kash: 'Conversation'.

jokes

Tia: So you have to copy me. (Singing) You're my honey bun, sugar plum . . . Now it's your go.

Theo: You're my honey bun, sugar bum.

Tia: No, you're my honey bun, sugar plum.

Theo: You're my honey bun, sugar bum.

Tia: Plum.

Theo: Sugar bum.

Taysia: I do live very far away. I live in Wales. It doesn't mean I'm a whale, does it?

Jude A: I love the word 'interesting', and 'interest', and 'investigate'. And I like the word 'dysfunctional' and 'a bit douche' and 'dictionary'.

Look who's talking

Language is probably the single biggest developmental change we see in the four to six-year-olds on *Secret Life*, and within the four-year-olds we see the starkest differences between children with advanced language and children without.

So much of what was so funny and affecting in the previous chapter was down to their turns of speech and the language they were using, and the programme shows us the degree to which language is the cornerstone of so much social learning. So many useful skills flow from it, like making friends, understanding instructions, information and ideas, the ability to compromise, to turn things to your advantage and to win arguments.

Theo, what would you like your team to be called?
Theo: Rainbow Coloured of Golden Sun.

Some of the most interesting moments around language have occurred when one child tries to convince others to do what they want, otherwise known as the art of persuasion.

Enzo: You're not listening to me!
Layton: You're not listening to *me*!

Using language to assert, connect and persuade

The art of persuasion was in short supply one morning when two four-year-old boys were sitting outside and a simple disagreement over who should move over escalated until one shouted, 'You're not listening to me!' The other shouted back, 'You're not listening to *me*!' Back and forth it went five times like a panto – 'Oh yes he did', 'Oh no he didn't'.

It was funny because it touched the four-year-old in all of us who longs to shout 'You're not listening!' to anyone who won't hear our point of view, or who isn't taking us seriously or who is shouting us down. But as adults we know that it's not necessarily the best way to win the argument.

In the heat of the moment these four-year-olds have neither the capacity nor the desire to compromise. And they don't yet have the five or six-year-olds' ability to trade insults or the range of vocabulary to break the deadlock. Words may have momentarily failed Enzo, but this went totally against his run of form. Enzo was usually able to weave words in sophisticated ways. On the first morning he enlisted a group of children to help him build a complex system of ramps and tunnels, and when a few of them started to run amok he stopped play, saying, 'Everyone, listen. This was not installed for walking. It was installed for wheels. Alright?' It was commanding. You don't argue with Enzo.

67

And Enzo understood that language could be used to assert yourself in the group, and so when he introduced himself saying his favourite animal was the 'lion guard what protects the pride land from the hyenas' he not only impressed the other children with his knowledge but he connected with the children who also liked animals. Enzo used language to lead games, to enforce rules, he wasn't afraid to intervene in someone else's argument. And when asked what he and a group of boys had been building he answered in a flash, 'A postcard-making machine for birthdays.'

Enzo: That's the *Flying Scotsman*. It was the first locomotive to reach the speed of a hundred miles per hour. And he don't fly. And he's not Scottish!

And for sheer chutzpah, you have to admire the masterful way he engaged his classmates in an impromptu game of Musical Statues to compete for some chocolate coins. Not only did he instigate the game in the self-ordained role as master of ceremonies, he even provided the music, 'Dun-nah nuh-nah nuh-nah NUH . . .' The scientists were impressed.

Enzo understood the power of words to raise his status and to give himself agency and influence within the group. And he was not afraid to use that power, 'Put your hand up if you want to see that chick. Right. Put your hands down.'

As teacher Kate remarked, 'Looks like we've got competition.'

What's going on when we persuade others?

There has always been interest in what qualities are required to be an inspiring leader. Language, confidence and creativity appear very important for producing the right words at the right moment, but there are less obvious factors at play too. A recent study scanned the brains of those on the receiving end of inspirational speeches, to look at which brain regions were involved with processing the messages. Scientists found that the regions responding to a given speech appeared to vary according to whether the speaker was part of the follower's in-group or their out-group. Only when the speaker was perceived as part of the in-group did inspirational speeches stimulate networks for processing meaning. It is not, therefore, all about the words or even the way they are spoken. It seems that a would-be leader must also cultivate a sense of being part of the 'gang' before their words can inspire their followers.

Charlotte: Take your dog around here. Let's sign him in, okay? You haven't been here before . . . What's your dog's name?

Jack: Maggie.

Charlotte: And what's your name?

Jack: Maggie.

Charlotte: Is it the same as your dog?

The art of persuasion: beyond words

Charlotte made an impressive vet's receptionist for a four-year-old. And she had the language to inhabit the role. This gave her an enormous advantage when it came to inventing games. It was a sign of her friend Jack's progress during that week that he was able to join in her fantasy game, but he didn't quite share her range when it came to vocabulary.

It was this *range* in language skills within any year group that really surprised us. As well as savouring the advanced language skills of a child like Charlotte or Enzo, we were moved by the frustrations of children struggling to be understood when their language didn't yet match what they were trying to communicate.

When Theo first tried to attract Tyler's attention he said simply, 'Please talk to you' – it was clear to us but possibly not to Tyler. And as four-year-old Tia chased Jack around the playground, determined to teach him that his victory celebrations weren't appreciated, saying, 'You're just a horrible friend,' words failed him but he did the logical thing in the face of a personal attack – first he grunted, then he growled, then he screamed at her. As Jack's dad said, 'It does frustrate him if he can't find the words.'

So how do you get the things you want in life if you *don't* have fluent language skills? How do you make people stop and listen to you? We saw techniques ranging from brute force to raised voices to theatrical displays of bravado. But more effective were the composed and quieter approaches. If the art of persuasion amounts to getting people to fall in with your plans or *getting your own way*, we saw that it wasn't always about having the words, it was knowing how, and crucially *when*, to use them.

Kahana: NO! NO! NO! Don't open it!

One day we saw a really interesting example of a child who was thoroughly effective and commanding without recourse to sophisticated language. When a box of helium-

filled balloons was left in the classroom covered in red tape but with no instructions, four-year-old Kahana took it upon himself to police the group. A boy with a strong sense of right and wrong and a charismatic, commanding presence, he managed to persuade and enforce his opinions using few words but making maximum use of body language. Kahana was born at thirty-two weeks and possibly as a result of this his speech was delayed. But there's no misunderstanding him when he stands over the box and says, 'No! No! No! Keep it closed! No.' Finally, one of them gives Kahana the slip and the balloons are set free, but not before he has effectively kept the whole group in check for the best part of half an hour.

Daisy: I am so proud of myself.

And then there was Daisy, five years old and a year into reception. Daisy has cerebral palsy and she needs support to sit up. She doesn't have any cognitive impairment – she's a good reader and chats away with her friends at school – but her speech takes time to tune in to. The other children, who weren't used to the way she spoke or to seeing someone in a wheelchair, made assumptions about her, namely that she was younger than them. And some of them talked to her in a baby voice, 'Oh but you can't, Daisy, you're not old enough to walk.' One can only imagine how frustrating it must have been for her as people repeatedly assumed things about her that were simply wrong.

We saw this vividly played out one morning when Daisy tried to instigate an imaginary game of Mums and Dads. 'Jude, come here to Mummy,' she called out. 'Would you like to go and get some new glasses?' But language is a game of call and response and the two children she wanted to play with didn't pick up on either of these cues,

so she tried again: 'I'm having a baby, look. Feel!' For a third time no one responded. 'That's just your belt, that's just your belt, I think,' the other girl said, and because language was effortful for Daisy she'd had enough after three attempts and started to cry.

For language to be effective and persuasive it needs good listening skills too and in this instance the other children weren't prepared to stop and listen to Daisy. As Dr Wass reflected, the children stepped in to nurture Daisy and to mother her, 'but it's a friend that Daisy wants'.

So it was heartening, later in the week, to see Daisy on a par with the other children in a performance task that drew on language and creativity. Daisy, Jet and Lewis were given three objects – a length of hosepipe, a glow stick and a dustpan – and they had to incorporate these into a play of some kind. When they were ready, Daisy announced that we would be seeing a fairy tale and, sure enough, deep in the forest, a gang and a magician accidentally released a host of devilish animals, and a bear snatched a precious dustpan from Daisy's grasp and had to be wrestled to the ground before good triumphed over evil.

We often felt giddy with the speed at which these children moved from game to game. As a colleague said, 'It's as if they live their life in fast-forward.' But this was Daisy's opportunity to assert herself and show the children the ways she was similar to them, when previously the other children in her class had only seen the ways in which she was different. From then on she was able to engage her friends in many rewarding, imaginary games, and language was no longer an issue.

Leadership and language

We were interested in our six-year-olds' powers of
persuasion and to test this we asked the children to
choose a Leader for the Day on each of the five days
they spent together. The teacher left the room and
it was up to them how they approached it. Their
techniques were revealing and varied a great deal.

One of the tallest boys, Kash, who happened also
to be the youngest, started canvassing for support
straight away. 'Right, let me be the leader. Yeah? Okay,
I'm the leader. I'm the leader of Charlie. Yeah? We made
our deal, didn't we, Charlie?' But this proved ineffective
in the long run. And Elvin, who was very quiet at first,
began gradually to assert his natural authority, using
few words but using them effectively. His technique
was to ask questions. Early on he suggested that
perhaps popularity should be the device for choosing:
'Maybe it's the one who has the most friends . . . ?' He
didn't think much of Kash's idea of deciding by an
arm-wrestling competition, wondering instead, 'Or do
we have to see who is the quietest?'

At this point Elvin's friend Beatrice pointed out,
'If someone says, "Oh I want to be leader," and then
someone else says, "Oh I want to be leader," the way
to solve that is voting. And sometimes it's called a
democracy.'

Recognizing that some of the girls, like Beatrice,
had found Kash's brute force and machismo off-
putting, Elvin asked simply, 'Who wants to vote for
me?'

His quiet approach, his morality and fairness won
him all the votes except one; Kash voted for himself.
To be fair, he immediately accepted the result, stepping
into the self-appointed role of deputy as he ordered

What skills do leaders have?

The research shows that two important qualities of a leader are, first, creativity and, second, the ability to focus on what's going on. These two qualities require quite different types of mental state, and possibly the real challenge is being able to move between them swiftly and seamlessly.

This is also suggested by the discovery of a network in the brain for mind-wandering. The 'default mode network' activates when we think about ourselves, or start day-dreaming about future possibilities. When this network is activated, it also means we are not paying much attention to what's happening around us – our external attention is limited while our internal attention holds sway. But, interestingly, our ability to fire up this network is helpful for our creativity. So, although it's important to be able to focus on the business at hand, it seems that the timely ability to go 'off-line' and day-dream occasionally may be an important part of being a leader too.

the others to listen to their new boss, Elvin, and, 'Follow the leader, follow the leader.' As Kash's mum said, 'He is a very dominant character, Kash is. He wants to be good but he can't help being a little bit rebellious.'

Spitfire versus Super Star Destroyer versus Twinkle Star

Elvin's use of language and qualities of leadership were impressive in a six-year-old, but we were fascinated to see that the skills for persuasive leadership were already present in some of our four-year-olds. It was remarkable to see demonstrations of effective teamwork and leadership at such a young age.

When five four-year-old boys were asked to build a

machine out of boxes *as a team* they each came up with something completely different. There was Joe, who wanted to build a Hawker Hurricane; Elliot, who wanted to build a Spitfire; Ivar, a Super Star Destroyer; Jack, a Laser Machine; and Theo, a Twinkle Star. In a brilliant bit of improvisation, teacher Ollie said, 'You've all suggested things that can fly.' Nevertheless, this was a tough circle to square.

To begin with, each boy doggedly held on to his own plan, even if all Jack really wanted to do was wrap himself up in Sellotape. But before long, one boy emerged as a natural leader. It was quietly done. He was fully focused on his own vision – the Spitfire – and he directed all his concentration to the task in hand. He laid out all the pieces he thought he would need and something about the quality of attention he brought to the task attracted the attention of the other boys. It was a case of leading by example. One by one the others fell in with his plan. They started asking him how much Sellotape he needed and where to put it. He'd barely said more than a few words, but people wanted to play *his* game. He was engineer in chief. Someone even offered to put some carpet in his cockpit.

We were all struck by this innate quality of leadership.

This was Elliot. He lives with his dad and older sister and he is interested in fixing things. He spends a lot of time in his bedroom and refers to it as his 'workshop'. His dad says, 'He instinctively understands how things work and how to fit them together.'

What made Elliot's build that day all the more remarkable was that he had taken some time to settle in with us. Two years earlier his mum had died of cancer, and when he first arrived Elliot was reluctant to leave his dad and come in and sit down with the other

children. He didn't want to join in with group activities at first.

As one of our psychologists, Dr Elizabeth Kilbey, explained, Elliot was working to hit all the same developmental milestones as the other children, 'but he's doing that in the context of trying to process and make sense of a huge emotional experience. That's a lot of work for a four-year-old.'

To begin with he took his beloved Bunny everywhere he went as a comforting, transitional object, helping him to bridge the gap between the safe environment of his home and this new and unfamiliar world he found himself in. Until the building task, that is, when Bunny was left on the steps.

Unsurprisingly, Elliot knew exactly what he wanted to be when he grew up: 'An inventor.'

Are leaders born or made?

Watching children of four, five and six as they acquire and use language skills is a fascinating and often very funny part of the show. Watching them use these skills as a way to persuade others and displaying qualities of leadership is nothing short of inspiring. We saw four-year-olds like Enzo, Charlotte and Elliot, five-year-olds like Daisy and six-year-olds Elvin and Beatrice demonstrate exceptional abilities to share and communicate their ideas, to motivate their friends, to encourage, to compromise and to harness support with real charisma and presence.

But leadership skills are not something you are born with necessarily, and we also saw many examples on the programme of children appearing to grow several inches taller as they discovered qualities in

What makes someone a good leader?

Our genetics have a significant influence on some of the skills needed for leadership, such as creativity. However, many aspects of leadership must be learnt. In particular, becoming a good leader depends on learning from the challenges you face, both in terms of your successes and your failures. This helps you accumulate a range of 'mental models' for different situations – which is not something you are born with. Being able to put different models together creatively can generate an entirely new vision for the future – something leaders such as Franklin Roosevelt and Nelson Mandela were able to do. It seems that to become a truly great leader, creativity and learning is required in droves.

themselves they didn't know they had when asked to take a leadership role – whether it was five-year-old Elijah succeeding in making the tastiest smoothie, four-year-old Taysia roaring like a lion at an imposter in the tree house, or five-year-old Harry leading his team to victory in a Memory Game.

And we saw that language didn't have to be the determining factor in making someone a good leader, and that the skills for leadership could be seen and encouraged in a four-year-old just as in a six-year-old.

And since the really great leaders are made not born, perhaps it's never too late to work on our own powers of persuasion and leadership skills.

What happens, Caitlyn, if someone doesn't do what you want them to do?
Caitlyn: In a game they would have to go to jail.

A guide to . . .

Find out about their background

Caitlyn: Are you a Muslim?

Marley: No.

Caitlyn: A Christian?

Marley: No, I'm nothing.

Caitlyn: I'm nothing either.

Marley: I'm just Jamaican and Scottish, I'm half Scottish and I'm half Jamaican.

Caitlyn: I'm half Japanese and half English.

Marley: You actually sound like you're half Japanese.

Reminisce about shared experiences

Elvin: I was born in St Thomas' Hospital.

Caspar: I was born in St Thomas'.

Elvin: It was so nice there, the comfy bed.

Caspar: I even had a TV.

conversation

Check you're both on the same page

Austyn: 'Idiotic' means 'idiot'.

Kash: Do you know what 'idiotic' means?

Kash: No it doesn't.

Austyn: Yeah it does.

Kash: Know what it actually means? F-U-K.

Austyn: The F-word . . . ?

Talk about the weather

Elouisa: Singing in the rain, what a glorious feeling.

Beatrice: It's raining, it's raining.

Caitlyn: If it's raining I'd better get my jacket.

Beatrice: But I love the rain.

Marley: Oh, this is the life isn't it?

Caitlyn: Yeah.

A guide to . . .

Discuss the journey

Emily: Go backwards and get on the pavement.

Alfie: I can't. It's stuck. The grass is stronger than the go-kart.

Discuss art

Caitlyn: (Painting) I don't want my mum to have arms. Or hands.

Kash: What!

Caitlyn: She doesn't deserve them since she's always on the phone.

conversation

Discuss food and travel

Nat: Do you know what people eat in France? Frog legs.

Ellie: Fox legs?

Nat: No, frog legs.

Calla: That's like a toad . . . in the hole. Toad is a type of frog. We are eating toad. We are eating frog.

Ellie: (To the teacher) Excuse me, I don't like this.

Discuss your hopes and dreams

Elouisa: Imagine if there was a massive paddling pool and someone put tea in it and we swam in tea.

feelings and what to do with them

Is it important to get stars and rewards? George: No. It's important what you feel inside.

One day the four-year-olds were playing a game outside. The children were in pairs and each pair was joined at the wrist by a few links of paper chain, like the ones you make at Christmas.

The object of the game was to play with your partner for as long as possible *without breaking the chain*. This wouldn't be an easy task for adults. For children of four it's a really big ask, requiring co-operation and compromise as well as an ability to keep your emotions in check. Too much excitement, high spirits or frustration would mean a broken chain.

One boy was reluctant to sit down while Kate, the teacher, explained the rules.

This was four-year-old Fabian, a gorgeous, animated, mischievous-looking boy who immediately charmed us all. His dad calls him The Arch Villain: 'When he's quiet, you're nervous and when he's not quiet you're nervous.'

And Fabian was in no mood for compromise. Within seconds he broke his own chain, much to his partner's annoyance. He discovered breaking the tether was fun and he went to find another couple chained at the wrist. His spirits rose as cries rang out from all sides of the playground, 'Chop! Chop! Chop!'

By the time Kate caught up with him he was wild with mischief and delight, and he refused to come to the side of the playground with her. In the end she had to remove him altogether and call time on his self-destructive rampage.

When Fabian was allowed back to the playground all the children had united against him. 'He's really not very nice to us, is he?' said one, and another, 'It's because he's

Why does it hurt to be left out?

The brain regions involved with processing social and physical pain overlap. This suggests some similarity in how we experience these two types of pain – and points to the important role our social life has played in our evolution. Feeling physical pain is helpful for knowing our bodies are at risk, but it seems it's been just as important for human survival to know when our emotional security is jeopardized.

naughty.' He tried to join in the games the other children were playing but he was systematically excluded.

As Professor Howard-Jones explains, 'From a neuroscience perspective, we know that the pain of being excluded from a social group activates very similar brain regions to physical pain, and I think you can see that here in Fabian. He's actually *hurting* from being excluded from the group.'

I don't have any friends . . .

Fabian wandered around the playground for a while watching the other children and then sat down on a step by himself and said under his breath, with a catch in his voice:

Emotional regulation

One of the hardest lessons we all have to learn when it comes to emotions is that expressing ourselves in the heat of the moment like Fabian did can have a dramatic impact on the people around us. Understanding this is the key to taking responsibility for our own feelings and not letting them spill over destructively. Scientists call it emotional regulation. The trouble is, there's no A-B-C of emotional regulation. It's another of those things we have to work out for ourselves, feeling our way towards our own set of

What is the tension between impulses and thinking?

Much of what we do – breathing, running, eating – can be done with very little involvement of the cortex, the wrinkly and best-known part of our brain most associated with conscious reasoning. A child who acts on impulse doesn't stop to engage his or her cortex and reason themselves out of the impulse – 'I might hurt someone', 'I might not get a reward later', 'I might annoy someone'. Somehow this child needs to slow down and engage this thinking part of the brain.

strategies contingent on our own personalities and circumstances, one step forward, two steps back. And this was the steep learning curve that our four, five and six-year-olds in *Secret Life* found themselves on as they made friends, fell out, made up, forgot they'd fallen out, forgave each other and moved on. Just watching them was an emotional roller-coaster.

Observing the children's intense relationships you see how emotional regulation varies from child to child and how much it impacts on their time on the programme. It is also the issue that adults tell us most frequently that they recognize in their own lives. There's something about watching a child unable to deal with their emotions that immediately brings to mind the adults we know who also struggle with this. And given the prevalence of road rage, online trolling, football hooliganism and more, it seems that mastering our emotions is a lifelong struggle.

At four to six years old we have some of the skills needed but others are still being learnt. When a five-year-old loses out on a medal and says, 'It's not fair to me, she has so many things. Look at her. I have nothing!' the outrage is raw and visceral. The way they express their emotions is not yet overlaid by manners or social convention, and this is what makes it so relatable; when

we see the children overwhelmed by fury, jealousy or self-destruction, ecstasy at winning, devastation at losing, we empathize; when we see the children struggling to keep their emotions in check, bursting with excitement, choking back the tears, swallowing their hurt pride or keeping a lid on the rage that's festering just below the surface, we feel it too.

The children in *The Secret Life of 4, 5 and 6 Year Olds* show us what a range of skills make up this complex and multi-faceted mechanism of emotional regulation. It isn't a simple accomplishment, like riding a bicycle: once mastered, never forgotten. It's more of a complicated mish-mash of skills and processes – some neurological, some psychological, some personality-driven – that together help us to experience our emotions to the full without letting them overwhelm us and dictate our behaviour.

What we do know is that language is key both in helping us communicate to others how we're feeling but also in processing emotions ourselves.

How does language help with our emotions?

Emotions are in-the-moment and intangible, but when we can give them a name we can bring them to mind more easily, and this means we can both talk and think about them when we're calmer and not boiling over with them. That may be why emotional understanding is strongly linked to language development.

By four years old, the potential for a 'virtuous circle' is already in full swing, such that children with greater language skills are learning more about the minds and feelings of others and this in turn is allowing them to communicate even more effectively. And friendships in which feelings are discussed are opening up new avenues of emotional support. Emotionally literate friends can help with reappraising a tricky situation and thinking about its meaning differently.

Tia: Erm, excuse me Miss, I'm so sorry what I have to do, but I have to pull your mum's baby out. I'm so sorry. Please give a chance. I will be very careful.

Take Tia, for example. Bubbly and assertive, she is the eldest of two and seems much older than her four years, although she still has the endearing look of a preschooler. From the minute she arrives she impresses us all with the way that she 'reads' social situations. Most of the children's emotional repertoire is fairly limited at this age – 'I hate you', 'I love you', 'I'm angry', 'I'm sad', 'fed up' – but not Tia's.

Playing Doctors and Nurses in what seems to be a maternity ward, Dr Tia talks with real feeling to the expectant mum, 'Erm excuse me Miss, I'm so sorry what I have to do, but I have to pull your mum's baby out. I'm so sorry. Please give a chance. I will be very careful.' Just a game, but it showed unusual empathy for a four-year-old nonetheless. And she was going to need all of her emotional maturity during her time with us.

Tia: Someone never said that to me before and now they have.

One morning two girls were playing on the slide, laughing as they held on to each other's back and slid down together. Tia asked if she could play but they said there wasn't enough room for three. This upset Tia and she asked her friend Nathaniel to come and talk to her 'alone' behind the slide. 'What should I do, Nathaniel, what should I do?' she said. Nathaniel clearly hadn't been asked such a thing before by another four-year-old, but he thought about it and said, 'You must say please can you go behind me?' Tia took his advice – another unusual skill in a four-year-old – and tried again. When she got the same response she said, 'Guys, guys, I'm just really sad because you didn't hold on to my back. And when I asked nicely you said "No".'

What happens next sounded brutal:

Charlotte: Well . . . no . . . it's cos I love her more.

Lola: She loves me more. You love me more, don't you?

Visibly stung, tears welled and Tia reached for her handkerchief to dab at her cheeks. 'You're making me sad,' she told them. She went to find the teacher, sobbing into her handkerchief, and found the words to describe what she was feeling: 'She said she loves Lola more. That really makes me upset. That really makes me sad. Someone never said that to me before and now they have. It's a really sad word.'

What is wonderful about this exchange, and particularly Tia's use of language, is that she distils the experience to its essence – 'it's a really sad word'. We don't know which word she means but we all know what she's talking about – that powerful feeling of rejection, upset and hurt when someone tells you they prefer someone else to you, as a friend, as a partner or for a job.

Impressive and heart-rending, it's also a brilliant lesson

Taylor: I like my blanket because it's soft. It keeps me safe. I can't sleep without it. And when there's monsters, I hide under it.

in social reasoning and emotional regulation: first label your feelings as accurately as you can, then have them acknowledged by someone in authority, accept an apology if it's on offer, and finally move on. In this instance Charlotte and Lola both apologized, and Tia went back and started playing happily on the slide with them.

Crucial in all this is the teacher's role in helping Tia to regulate and soothe herself. We were often transfixed by the way that teacher Kate would comfort a child who was upset. She didn't say much, sometimes all she did was repeat back what the child said to her while she rubbed their back, but in that moment we saw the transformative effect of simply listening to someone and acknowledging what they're feeling. It can shift overwhelming upset, rage or jealousy from something catastrophic back to more manageable proportions.

This reminds us again of something true throughout our lives. The natural impulse as an adult would be to shield a child from situations like this. But it's much more important for us to learn to process strong emotions, as Tia was able to here. And it's never too late to start trying to articulate how you feel, describing emotions as a first step towards reasoning with them.

At four years old we saw in Tia someone who was beginning to express the full range of her emotions. When she's asked what it's like having a baby sister, she said without hesitation:

It's like a dream come true . . . and a nightmare.

When do emotions start?

In the first few months after birth, infants distinguish emotions in others in only the simplest of ways. However, each step of emotional development offers a deepening of their interaction with others and a better 'platform' for learning more. By three months old, infants can discriminate between happy and angry faces, but by one year they can use others' faces to guide their decisions. By two years children have a sense of self-awareness – that they are separate and independent from others. This opens the door to understanding that others have thoughts and feelings that may be different from their own, and the possibility of thinking about what these might be. At three years children are learning how to take turns and play interactively, which creates many more opportunities to see the consequences of their own actions for others. Children are becoming increasingly able to be more friendly and helpful to those who appear to be friendly themselves, and bonds are beginning to form.

By four years old, children may still be struggling to regulate their own strong emotions, but they are also discovering how to make their friends laugh – that some types of interaction produce better results than others – and they are beginning to empathize with how their friends might be feeling and why.

In subsequent years the connections between brain centres underneath the cortex that are important for emotional response, such as the amygdala, increase their connectivity to regions of our cortex that support our emotional reasoning. As we interact with and learn from others, the extent of these connections reflects our emotional literacy, and we become more capable of identifying and reasoning about our own feelings and those of others.

How do feelings change?

How many emotions does the average four, five or six-year-old have in their repertoire? A well-known parenting website lists over 300 emotions that an older child may

Lola: I'm a little bit worried if Mummy had another baby. So it'll be me, Mabel, the new baby *and another baby*. So I'm a little worried if I can't fit in that house.

experience, everything from ambivalent and astounded to jealous and jumpy to worried and worn down. Truth is, there are an infinite number of emotions – the only limit is having the language to describe them. Intriguingly, there are far fewer positive feelings on the list than negative ones, probably because positive emotions are easier to deal with – when we feel relaxed or affectionate or joyful we are less likely to need a coping mechanism than when we feel anxious, angry or upset.

So how does this change as the children get older?

Feelings at four years old

In the programme our four-year-olds feel things strongly but label them simply – words like 'sad', 'mad', 'love', 'hate' crop up a lot – and they are learning to label those feelings, as Tia did so eloquently in the playground. By four they have already learnt some social conventions – 'say sorry', 'say please', 'don't grab' – but they can't always put them into practice. Simply put, until they've developed fully the idea that other people have a mind, things like please and sorry don't really make sense. At four they can begin to distinguish between what they feel inside (their internal emotions) and their actions (the outward expression of them), and they are gradually understanding that alongside *external* soothing mechanisms, like a parent or caregiver, they have their own *internal* self-soothing techniques. And they are beginning to grasp the hardest lesson – that for every action there's a reaction, and that their actions will have consequences, not just for themselves but for other people too.

Many psychologists are now looking into the positive reinforcement of good emotions and whether we can train ourselves to sustain a happier state of mind if we concentrate as much on positive as negative feelings. Luckily the cast of *Secret Life* are on hand to give us a few tips. For example, when five-year-old Emily said, 'This is the best day of my life,' in response to being given five stars for kindness by the teacher, she's noticing the intensity of just how good she feels, and psychologists suggest she may well be enhancing that feeling just by giving voice to it.

Voicing their own and other people's feelings happens in all sorts of different circumstances. When four-year-old Lola sees her younger sister, Mabel, struggling and finally dissolving in tears as she tries to build a tower with sticks, Lola says to her: 'I've had a lot of practice to make castles and do you know what? Eventually one day I got it. You just have to keep trying, see? That's how I learnt.'

Mabel was cheered by Lola's encouragement and set about helping her team with their castle saying, 'When I cry she makes me happy again.'

Later Lola reflected, 'It's just a really nice thing to do, to "courage" people. It's a bit like in *The Wizard of Oz* when the cowardly lion's lost his courage.'

Of course it's a mutually beneficial arrangement to help your friends, because one person gets comfort or encouragement while the other is able to hone their social skills and their empathy. Whether they always choose to use it is another matter.

Mabel: Is the sheep going to eat me?

Lola: No Mabel, they're friendly.

Mabel: Well sheep bite me all the time.

Lola: No they don't. We've never even been near sheep.

Chaim: Here you go. It's the wrong way round. Skyla. I am sorry. From Chaim. And then I done a rabbit. That's a bunny rabbit. Skyla: Why? Why did you draw a bunny? Chaim: Because it's your favourite animal.

Saying sorry

It's at around this age that sorry stops being just a word and we start to understand the meaning behind it. Chaim, who we saw earlier taking the chocolate from Skyla, wanted to make amends by drawing Skyla a picture of her favourite animal, a touching, empathetic gesture of friendship. Okay, so she doesn't quite get it when she's given the card, but that doesn't matter because Chaim turned a moment of impulse into what teachers call 'an opportunity for growth'.

We could all take a leaf out of Chaim's book. He owned up, he tried to made amends by saying sorry and doing something really kind, and in the process he was able to forgive himself and move on, having learnt a valuable lesson – to wait for the answer next time he asks someone for a piece of chocolate!

Feelings at five years old

At five years old the palette is becoming more varied and subtle. They still feel things just as intensely and their feelings can still spill over in operatic proportions. But we see some really good techniques for self-soothing and some more effortful, purposeful internal strategies for keeping overwhelming feelings at bay – be it singing a song, talking to oneself or simply having some time alone. We also see five-year-old friends starting to help each other cope with difficult feelings, and it's impossible not to be touched by these shows of empathy and caring.

Like a true friend Jet supports Nat when her team beats his team at football:

What did Jet say or do?

Nat: She made me feel very happy. She made me feel *Ar ben y byd*.

What does *Ar ben y byd* mean?

Nat: It's 'On top of the world' in Welsh.

And look at this demonstration of how friends can help us cope with difficult feelings. Five-year-old Calla wins a cuddly toy called Bert in one of the challenges, only to find that her best friend, Ellie-Mae, wanted the very same dog, which leaves Calla feeling 'super sad'. Jet spots that Calla is upset and asks what's up:

Jet: Calla . . . why are you sad?

Calla: Because Ellie-Mae wants to take the dog that I won.

Jet: She did want it really much and it's sad, but *you* don't need to be sad. You can take this home but you don't need to be sad. Okay?

Calla: I'm sad because she was a friend and now she's not.

Jet: But you can be my friend.

Calla: Thank you, Jet.

Jet's brilliantly straightforward, logical approach to the situation, together with her acknowledgement of everyone's feelings, helps Calla to feel better and they start comparing wobbly teeth.

But as we saw from time to time, when all else fails, throwing a tantrum is always an alternative strategy.

Jude: I'm NOT out!

When Jude point-blank refuses to accept that he has been called out in a game of Musical Statues his friends are bemused, and even a bit amused. As Jude stamps his feet and wails, 'But why . . . I tried my best and I'm still out!' one of the other children remarks, 'We just play fun. It's just a game.' To be fair Jude had attempted a cartwheel – a high-risk strategy – and he had got caught with his legs in the air.

Psychologists will tell us that anger *can* be a positive force for good if we can only harness it. In *The Secret Life of 4, 5 and 6 Year Olds* we saw histrionic displays of floor-bashing, fist-pounding, feet kicking, fake crying, real crying, shouting and mayhem and destruction. If we have difficulty regulating our emotions, we can feel so angry

What is happening when we get angry?

Most of the negative feelings we experience, such as fear, sadness and disgust, cause us to move away from the thing that causes them, while most of the positive emotions (like happiness and surprise) cause us to approach. Anger doesn't fit this pattern. With anger the impulse is to become more involved with the situation that has evoked it. And it can lead to a temporary increase in testosterone, and impulses towards aggression, dominance and competition.

The anger response is believed to help us defend ourselves when we are threatened, and it can occur alongside a fight-or-flight response. When the brain registers a threat, the adrenal glands flood the body with stress hormones such as adrenalin and cortisol. In this way, the brain is responding by shunting blood away from the gut and towards the muscles, in readiness for any physical exertion that might be needed. The actions of the heart and lungs can also increase, together with flushing and shaking.

that the surge of hormones we experience can leave us feeling 'beside ourselves'. In other words, our behaviour can feel so out of our control that it's as if someone else is pulling our levers.

We talk about the 'terrible twos' as though tantrums are something you grow out of, but on the programme our biggest tantrums have all been thrown by five-year-olds.

When do tantrums stop?

Feelings at six years old

Our sample of children was small, but it was interesting nevertheless that we didn't see any tantrums from our six-year-olds. When Kash missed out on being Leader of the Day all week, and really minded, he didn't throw a tantrum but instead took himself off to the Wendy house, asking, 'Why isn't no one my friend here?' And when one team of six-year-olds lost after three heated rounds of Tug of War they supported each other rather than getting mad at the winners, as our four or five-year-olds might have done. Is this because the six-year-olds had perfect mastery of emotional regulation? Almost certainly not, but maybe their greater self-consciousness and social awareness were helping the group, and individuals within it, to regulate themselves.

Elvin: Yeah, but I thought I was Beatrice's best friend?

At six a more complex and nuanced set of emotions is starting to kick in, including the urge to cover up one's true feelings, and the six-year-olds have the language

97

skills to describe these feelings. We held Beatrice and Elvin's friendship up as one based on shared interests and styles of play. Unexpectedly, Beatrice found herself more and more attracted to the boisterous games being played by Elouisa and there was a powerful attraction of opposites between the two girls. When Elvin was asked how he felt about Beatrice playing Kiss Chase with Elouisa, he was unconvincing when he said, 'Happy. So Beatrice has more friends.' And if we were in any doubt, listen to his true feelings a little later when Beatrice was asked why she shared her gold coins with Elouisa:

> Beatrice: Best friends.

> Kash: What? No, you're not.

> Beatrice: Yes.

> Elvin: Yeah, but I thought I was Beatrice's best friend?

Beatrice's new best friend jeopardized her strong friendship with Elvin and Elvin nursed his wounds, muttering, 'It's not fair,' as the girls ate their sweets. Later on when Beatrice described Elvin as her 'second best friend', it was impossible not to feel that sting of rejection.

Payback time came when Beatrice's team lost an important game and Elvin celebrated his team's victory right in her face. They found themselves all square, but having lost each other's friendship. But the way it turned out was confirmation of Elvin and Beatrice's real emotional competence. It didn't take long before they realized how much they missed each other's humour and sensibility, not to mention the 'good games', and Elvin knew he needed to make a sincere apology and suggest an activity that could repair their damaged friendship.

Seeing difficult emotions impact friendships in real and painful ways and then seeing those friendships repaired

Elvin: Beatrice, do you want to help me make my Minecraft book?

Beatrice: Yeah Minecraft! Maybe we could make a Minecraft world?

Elvin: Yes!!! That's a great idea, Beatrice. Come on, let's go tell Kate.

with real emotional intelligence was one of the most touching aspects of working with the six-year-olds. Would Elvin and Beatrice's friendship have struck such a chord with viewers, I wonder, if not for the emotional hoops they had to jump through in order to cement the special bond they had with each other?

What's abundantly clear from our fours, fives and sixes is that while emotional regulation is a steep developmental learning curve, we don't start at the beginning, tick off milestones along the way and arrive at the finishing line. For most of us it is a work in progress. And like so many other areas of social interaction in *Secret Life*, learning to deal with one's feelings is more of a continuum than a series of dots to be joined up.

These children are making huge strides and the joy is seeing how they respond to and learn from each other when it comes to regulating their feelings. Accepting and valuing other children's emotions helps them to accept and value their *own* emotions. This is true for four, five and six-year-olds but it's also true throughout our lives. Accepting and valuing our own emotions helps us not only *feel* better, it also helps us to *do* better, in all aspects of our lives.

Can we ever separate thoughts and feelings?

The neuroscience of emotions emphasizes how much our feelings are bound up with our thoughts – to the extent that many scientists consider that they cannot be studied separately. The huge role emotions play in our development points to the fundamental importance of knowing our feelings and understanding them. At the same time, the waves of powerful hormones that emotions can release remind us of the need to regulate our feelings to avoid them entirely controlling us. Letting in our emotions but preventing them from taking over can be a tricky balancing act, whatever our age.

A guide to . . .

Don't talk down to a six-year-old

Caitlyn: These people sound like they're from reception.

Jayda: We are not in reception.

Caitlyn: You don't really act like you're six, six-year-olds wouldn't push, they would just wait.

Don't insult someone else's taste

Cuba: I'm making a fireplace but mine's better than yours. Look at my fireplace. Yours is rubbish.

Christian: It's not nice to say other people's things are rubbish. It's not really nice to say that.

Cuba: Both of ours are good. Okay. Both of ours are good.

Don't hold back

Maimoona: I will punch him in the face when I get strong.

managing your emotions

Label feelings

George: I hate you. I wish I had a better brother.

Calla: I felt super-sad.

George: Jack was sad because he lost against me, so I was thinking, you know what, I'll just give him a sweet.

Voice positive feelings

Nat: Dear Calla, I like you.

Emily: This is the best day of my life.

Harry: (After winning Penalty Shoot Out) My head's going to blow up.

Get a little help from your friends

Channel your favourite superhero when you're upset

Jack: I wanna be Hellboy!

Lola: Keep trying, Mabel. We're sisters – sisters forever.

Mabel: I don't want to be sisters forever. I just want to be sisters.

A guide to . . .

Sing it if it's too hard to say it

Have a good cry

Lola: (Singing) I miss my dad . . . but you don't want to be my friend.

Tia: (Singing) I want to be alone.

Taylor: (Singing) I miss my mummy. She's so beautiful. And I miss her. It doesn't matter . . .

Lola: (Singing) All I need is my best friend's love. All I need is my friend, Alicia. That's the only friend I need.

Taylor: Can you stop singing those songs. I feel nervous.

Alfie: My tears was running down my cheeks but I was just washing my eyes out, that's all.

managing your emotions

Develop strategies for calming yourself down

George: I just like being on my own.

Oliver: Guys, just go away.

Oscar: But I'm your best buddy.

Nat: (singing) Maybe far away, or maybe real nearby . . . They'll be there calling me baby, maybe.

Oliver: Just go away, I know I'm a sucker, just go away!

girls and boys

What do you think the difference is between girls and boys?

Caspar: Er, when boys grow up, sometimes they have beards or moustaches, girls don't have some. But my grandma, she has a moustache.

Through the many episodes of *The Secret Life of 4, 5 and 6 Year Olds* the subject of gender has surfaced again and again, provoking our scientists to heated discussion and debate. Why did the girls resist the chocolate cake but not the boys? Why did the boys cheat in the beanbag race while the girls followed the rules? Why were the boys more willing to risk their winnings?

It's a contentious area, and there's still much academic disagreement as to which differences are innate and the role of biology in talking about gender. When scientists talk about 'male and female' they are talking about biological differences. When we talk about 'gender', we're talking about a construct, an *interpretation* of what it means to be male or female. And of course any discussion of differences between the genders at this age can say just as much about our different expectations of, and responses to, boys and girls as it does about innate differences between them.

But given how significant these questions around gender difference are, we couldn't ignore them. And so, in a departure for *Secret Life*, we set up a more pointed social experiment, playing a number of games that explored gender difference explicitly. And our attempts to see what differences there might be in behaviour led to some of our most-loved and memorable exchanges.

We undertook this 'experiment' with a group of children who had already spent a year at school, our five-year-olds. In week one, nine boys came to play and did a series of tasks and challenges for half the week, and then nine girls replaced the boys for the second half of the week. And although far from laboratory conditions, the girls and boys had the same playroom, same toys and same tasks. How would they compare? In the second week we brought them together and observed how they collaborated on some mixed-gender tasks. The results were as surprising as they were revealing.

Who cheats more? Girls or boys?
Charlotte, four: Probably boys.
Why is that?
Charlotte: Because they're more like . . . boyishy.

The Lemonade Test

We set up an experiment one summer's day in which the teacher offered the children homemade lemonade, emphasizing that it was homemade and that she had made it especially for them. The only problem was she had made it with salt. It's a classic test of empathy. We wanted to see if the way girls and boys reacted would be at all different.

First, three boys, Elijah, Harry and Oliver, all excited to be getting such a special treat, but immediately they scrunched up their faces in disgust:

Elijah: Oh no! That is disgusting!

Harry: It's too sweet and I'm gonna be sick tonight.

107

Oliver: I can't have any more. It's so disgusting.

Harry: It makes me sick.

Oliver: I just don't wanna drink it.

So far, so brutally honest.

Then it was the turn of the girls, Siena, Alice and Tiara. Their teacher poured them a glass each as well; they each took a sip, they registered the taste of the salt, but then they quickly collected themselves. Five-year-old Siena said, 'It was a teeny bit too much lemon.' Alice added, 'I love the lemon inside it,' and with that they began to tell a pack of fibs:

Siena: I think it's incredible, but I don't like the lemon in it.

Tiara: I loved it, but I didn't like the lemon, the other lemon in it.

Alice: Even though that I like it, please can I just have a drink of water?

Later on, Tiara admitted, 'I was pretending I did like it so it made her happy.'

Our scientists were delighted. We know that, according to the research, there's a marked difference in levels of empathy between boys and girls of this age. As early as

three to four months old, girls have been shown to outperform boys at responding to a range of facial expressions. And empathy – or the ability to take another's perspective and respond accordingly – relies on precisely this sort of skill. In fact, empathy is the clearest example of a sex difference that carries across the span of our lives. So seeing the girls prioritize the teacher's feelings over their own in our Lemonade Test was in keeping with current research.

Are male and female brains different?

There are some differences between girls' and boys' brains that can be identified from birth. For example, in general, the left and right hemisphere of a girl's brain appear to be more similar than those of a boy's, and boys also appear to have greater volumes of grey matter. It seems clear that from the outset there are sex differences in how the brain is developing. There is likely to be a link between these brain differences and the tendency of four-year-old girls to have better social reasoning skills, empathy, fine motor skills and language. However, working out the details of this link remains an ongoing challenge for scientists.

A guide to . . . what boys think of girls

Caspar: Disgusting. The look of them is so disgusting.

Layton: Girls are gooder.

Elvin: When I see girls I always think, 'Here we go again, marriage comes.'

Can girls be strong?

What good things can girls do?

Jude: No way, because they can only lift up a little tiny ant.

Elvin: Cooking, hovering, laundry, washing up.

A guide to . . .
what girls think of boys

Alice: Boys are smelly.

Siena: And they do stinky farts.

Amelia: Some boys bully girls and some girls bully boys.

So do you like boys, Naomi?

Naomi: Yeah, love 'em.

Are there any differences between language ability in girls and boys?

Recent studies have confirmed that the spoken language ability of boys does indeed lag behind girls, but the differences are not as great as once reported in the 1970s, possibly due to cultural changes in our society. At around two years, boys only lag by an average of around one month behind girls. These differences can be more noticeable to parents at four years old, when many children have their first opportunity to socialize together in large groups as their parents look on, but by six or seven years old the average differences are difficult to detect. However, there is also a greater range of ability among young boys than among girls, with more instances of boys' language development causing parental concern. This may explain why the average difference between boys' and girls' language ability is often thought to be greater than it actually is.

When the girls and boys were kept apart

The differences were evident from the minute the girls and boys arrived in the play centre. Bear in mind that none of these children had met one another before, so any same-sex peer pressure was generated there and then within the room. The boys immediately occupied the space; two of them pretended to be dinosaurs, one was a zombie and the others did some press-ups. By contrast, the girls sat down straight away; one of them introduced herself quite formally to the rest of the group, and they started comparing and complimenting each other, using all their social skills to interact and get to know each other. The boys, by this time, had started to wrap up the playroom in several metres of wool.

When they were invited to introduce themselves with a teacher in the room, the boys picked out tangible qualities – 'I'm tall', 'I'm strong', 'I'm brave' – defining themselves by their physical prowess. One said he had a lot of money in his piggy bank. Harry said he was always hungry. The girls by contrast picked out their social attributes and interpersonal skills; one said she was kind and helped other people, another that she had a lot of friends.

Both boys and girls were quickly attracted to the make-up we'd left out in the Home Corner. The girls imitated what they had seen other people do, administering eye shadow and lipstick with the precision of fully fledged make-up artists. The boys went for a freestyle approach – more warpaint than contouring – free of social constraints and stereotypical role models.

> Alice: I have two boyfriends. And they're both cats.

> Harry: I want to tell you something. I have twenty girlfriends.

> Teacher: Oh wow!

> Harry: But it wasn't me who asked 'em. They asked me and I didn't have a choice.

Naomi: Make sure you look magnificent for the party, okay?

When we tested a piece of research in the context of this experiment, we were often surprised by how closely our small cohort backed up the findings or received wisdom, as with the Lemonade Test. Draw Your Home was based on research suggesting that girls tend to emphasize people in their drawings of their homes, while boys focus more on the physical and structural design of the buildings. We were amazed to see one girl put a figure in every window of her three-storey house, another draw

herself and her mum at the front door and a third girl draw all the children in their beds, while one of the boys drew the garden shed in some detail, another the brick path up to the front door and another specified that the front door was made of wood. There was not a person in sight in the boys' drawings.

But inevitably there were surprises too, as our boys and girls bucked stereotypes and expectations. Our scientists thought the girls would shine in tasks that relied on good communication skills, given what we know about girls being ahead of boys at this age when it comes to vocabulary and language skills.

We played a Memory Game, the one where you unveil twenty objects on a tray and have to remember as many as you can. The best technique is to name each of the objects and discuss them with your team, thereby committing them to verbal memory. Our scientists predicted that the girls would outperform the boys. And the girls did well. But then along came five-year-old Harry – albeit a reluctant team captain – who labelled each object and then demonstrated near perfect recall on behalf of his team.

In another game, called Build the Tallest Tower, we thought the need for good teamwork and communication skills might give the girls the edge, but we hadn't reckoned on an exceptional team leader in five-year-old Oscar. Oscar was able to communicate his vision – 'Let's build the tallest tower!' – while keeping his whole team focused on the job in hand, 'Try and never give up,' and motivating them to succeed, 'That's a good epic idea,' and, 'Good going, guys, good,' showing masterful use of language and exceptional collaborative skills.

However, gradually we saw quite formalized styles of play emerging in the same-sex groups, to the point that anyone who wanted to play differently began to stand out. Children like Alice. It was Alice who, when the girls and boys were comparing how many girlfriends and boyfriends

Alice: Would you like to play dinosaurs with me?

Maryam: Please can we play Baby Baby.

they each had, announced that she had two 'and they're both cats'. During the girls-only days, we watched Alice build a remarkable structure all on her own, with an engineering precision and sense of design that impressed our scientists. She was keen to play with the bricks and the dinosaurs 'like she did at home with her friends Jake, Logan, Lewis, Harvey, Anthony and Christopher.'

But however enticing she tried to make it sound, her fellow girls only had eyes for the dolls, the doll strollers and the dressing up. Alice knew a lot about dinosaurs but she commented wistfully, 'The girls wouldn't play dinosaurs with me because they thought it was a boys' game.'

Alice: Do you know a T-rex? Its teeth is as big as a banana.

When do we become male or female?

Sex differences are thought to begin a few weeks after conception when, for around half of us, genes for maleness will set to work. These genes define whether testicles or ovaries will emerge. These organs produce different levels of hormones such as testosterone and oestrogen, helping to shape our unborn brain in sex-specific ways. There is also another surge in sex hormones after birth that peaks at around one month – a period scientists now refer to as a 'mini-puberty'. Hormone levels then can predict behaviours later in early childhood. For example, greater language ability is predicted by lower testosterone levels shortly after birth. This can help explain why girls tend to be ahead of boys in language at around four years old. Amazingly, hormone levels during mini-puberty can also predict whether a girl is more likely to play with a boy-typical toy. Clearly, biology is a major player in shaping the brains of boys and girls. This shaping begins before contact with cultural ideas of what being a boy or girl might mean.

A guide to . . .
what girls think of girls

Siena: They are more gentle and kind.

Elisa: Girls have bigger brains than boys.

What's important for girls when they grow up?

Siena: I'm an expert at girls.

Eva: To go to work and vote, definitely. Girls used to not vote, then there were these girls who fighted to vote, they were very silly women, cos they got killed, so it's very important for girls to vote, otherwise that will happen again.

Lola: I know the girls are never going to win. The boys always have bigger brains and the girls always have smaller.

A guide to . . .
what boys think of boys

Harry: They wear awesome clothes and they are just so awesome.

Jude R: We are super smart and super cool and super handsome.

Do you think boys should get to wear nail varnish and make-up if they want to?

Nat: Yes and I think they should play with dolls more oftenly.

Is it okay for men to cry?

Jude A: Only if their hearts are breaking.

What do you think about boys marrying boys?

Caspar: They have no children. But they'll still be happy. They might be boyfriend and boyfriend.

Christian: I'm not your boyfriend and you're not my boyfriend. Boys can't be boyfriends.

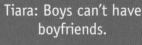

Tiara: Boys can't have boyfriends.

Elijah: Yeah, boyfriends can have boyfriends, because they're a boy and they're a friend.

Putting stereotypes to the test

Some previous studies have found that in games involving risk, adolescent boys will focus on the potential gain and girls on the chances of winning, making girls more risk-averse than boys. We wanted to test this out with our five-year-olds and so we challenged the boys and then the girls to a Penalty Shoot Out contest and offered the winners – one boys' team and one girls' team – the opportunity to double their prize or risk handing it over to the losing team. In the event, the boys took the gamble and ended up losing their prize, while the girls stuck with their sweets to share out agreeing, 'Let's not, just in case we lose.'

Our teams played exactly to type – the boys kept their eye on the prize and lost, the girls weighed the odds and decided not to take the risk. On this occasion the girls' approach paid off, but there are times in life when ignoring the odds is the only way to go, and researchers in this field point out that careful risk analysis (more often associated with women) can be a blessing and a curse.

Harder to put to the test, though plain to see in the kind of gendered play-styles that were emerging, was the extent to which the children had already absorbed gender stereotypes and conditioning from the world around them. A few years ago there was a successful viral campaign called #LikeAGirl, in which a well-known sanitary pad brand showed that around puberty girls begin to downgrade their abilities in favour of boys. When young women were asked to throw a ball *like a girl* they threw it feebly and when they were asked to run *like a girl* it was with arms and legs akimbo. In a homage to this experiment we were

curious to find out to what extent our five-year-olds already held ideas like this in their heads. We asked our children to perform a number of similar actions – to walk, to run, to pose, to laugh, to throw and to catch – as if they were the opposite sex. And to repeat these actions as their own sex.

What we discovered was that stereotypical ideas, beliefs and prejudices about the opposite sex were dismayingly alive and kicking at five years old. We watched as the girls roared and muscle-pumped while acting as boys but this was nothing to the boys who flounced and whinnied down the grass like a bunch of animated Barbie dolls. Most alarming was a demonstration of peer pressure in action as the boys saw each other's performance and adapted their own to fit in, always veering further towards the stereotype rather than drawing back from it. Regrettably this chimed with research suggesting that by age six strong gender stereotypes are already well entrenched.

Jude R: Girls act like this, 'Hello, I'm pretty.' Naomi: Smell my muscles. Jude R: Oh my God, my boobies hurt.

As Dr Kilbey remarked, 'These children were not born with these ideas, they're not innate, they've learnt them from the world they've grown up in. And research shows that the ideas these children have around gender are going to stay with them into their adult lives.'

Fortunately, when the five-year-old girls were asked to run 'as girls' they set off down the track like the athletes they were, no hint of any derogatory flounces or bounces. The scientists cheered.

What is happening in the brain with stereotypes?

Children quickly learn to create their own culture, with its own rules, traditions and ideas. The tendency of four and five-year-olds to self-segregate into same-sex groups creates a situation that can easily breed gender stereotypes. Children and adults are more likely to revert to stereotypes about the opposite sex when the opposite sex is not present.

Although stereotypes are easily formed, they can be difficult to entirely lose. Brain imaging has revealed that when we learn a new way of looking at things, the old way doesn't entirely disappear. The brain activity for the old idea can still be seen alongside that for the new idea. Instead of our old thinking being 'erased', it seems part of acquiring a fresh perspective is learning to suppress the old one. When it comes to sex differences and gender, the stereotypes we first learnt as children may never be far away!

When do gender stereotypes set in?

According to current research, children start to show a preference for same-sex peers around three years old. This is known as 'gender segregation'. This steadily increases until about six and then remains stable until the onset of adolescence.

We noticed with our four, five and six-year-olds that if a girl and a boy were asked to pick teams they would often segregate along gendered lines and form strong in- and out-groups based on gender, cemented by chants and taunts: 'Come on girls', 'The girls are going to whip it', 'The boys are cheating' and so on.

When six-year-old Caitlyn formed her 'Girls' Club', she was adamant that it would do just what it said on the tin, no boys allowed.

It is generally accepted that children's concepts of other people's gender and their own become increasingly

stable and consistent – this is known as 'gender constancy' – and between three and six years old children begin to form stereotypes about physical features and activities (for example, girls wear dresses and boys play with trucks). Again, we saw evidence for this amongst our five-year-olds.

When the girls and boys were brought together

After the first week apart we brought the five-year-old girls and boys together for the second week, and instantly they fell into some pretty familiar and stereotypical roles; the boys claimed they'd trashed the place, the girls accused them of being loud and messy and said they weren't going to clear up after them. And there were propositions, 'I was wondering if you could be a boyfriend with me, please?'

In order to mix things up a bit we decided to play a Dressing Up Game. In 2009 a photographer called J.J. Levine took a series of prom photos, two photos for each couple, one photo showing the couple in their finery and another once the couple had *reversed* their clothes and their 'gender' – girls dressed as boys, boys dressed as girls. The resulting pairs of pictures are strange and intriguing; you peer at them looking for essential 'boy-ness' and 'girl-ness', trying to work out who's who. Without clues as to the subject's lived gender, you can't find anything stable or consistent to help you 'read' the photos.

The children took happily to the idea of a competition for the Best-Dressed Couple, wasting no time slipping into tux, top hats and dresses. 'I'm gonna look like the smartest person in the world,' crows Jude. 'You won't look smart if you don't wear a moustache,' says Siena.

But when the bombshell was dropped that they must

now swap outfits they were horrified: 'I have to be a girl, really?' 'I can't believe I have to put a girly dress on.' The girls had fewer reservations about cross-dressing, but the boys were ridiculed and laughed at – not by the girls but by other boys. Gradually their defences were worn down, and besides they fancied getting their hands on some of that make-up again.

Alice, five: Oh wait girls, stop. Good news, I just remembered something. We need to go first, you know why? Because we're dressed up as boys.

The scientists wanted to encourage the children to think about what it actually means to be a boy or a girl and to gently explore the idea that, while we are born into one sex or another, our gender involves conscious decisions. We all make choices about how we identify ourselves and the clothes we wear give out loud signals to the world. Some free play that followed the dressing up demonstrated this emphatically. Still in their bow ties and waistcoats, the girls were pushing two beautiful boys – dressed as girls – on the roundabout until Alice looked down and said, 'Oh wait girls, stop. Good news. I just remembered something. We need to go first, you know why? Because we're boys.'

The idea behind bringing the boys and girls *together* was to explore current thinking on the advantages of mixed-gender groups. 'At the age of five,' our psychologist Dr Alison Pike explained, 'mixed-gender groups benefit boys and girls by allowing them to learn about the other sex, to break down gender stereotypes and to understand themselves within the social world.'

How much is nature and how much nurture?

Although the development of our gender begins with our biology, it certainly doesn't end there. Experience impacts on how gender-typical our behaviour is, and the experiences offered to boys and girls can be very different. Irrespective of size and weight, newborn daughters appear more likely to be described as 'little' and 'cute' than newborn sons. Parents generally tend to spend more time trying to communicate verbally with their infant daughters than sons, tend to provide their children with gender-typical toys and will believe their infant boys are capable of greater physical feats than they actually are. So while girls are born with a head start for language, their experiences following birth have the potential to reinforce this. However, accumulating experience helps boys to catch up until the difference tends to disappear at around six years old. The early and enduring cultural difference between the world of boys and girls makes it difficult to disentangle the nature and nurture of sex differences.

Oscar, five: Boys are stronger than girls. Well, girls can be strong, it's cos that they have to take lessons.

Jude and Eva

We were consciously looking for examples of boys and girls learning things from each other and perhaps unlearning some other ideas in the process. Nowhere was this clearer than when Eva – a brown belt in karate – took on Jude – 'my boobies hurt'. Jude is the youngest of two boys and from the minute he arrived he played the joker making everyone laugh with his celebration dances, his moonwalk and goofy faces. 'He does get away with a lot because he's Jude,' according to his mum, 'he's got the cute face and he's so friendly, he'll speak to anybody.' His nan and grandad tease him, asking if he's got a girlfriend, but he's adamant, 'No, no, no, I don't have a girlfriend.'

We gave Eva the task of teaching Jude some of her moves. Earlier in the week Jude had made some remarks about girls:

> Why can't girls be scientists?

> Jude: Because they make silly potions.

> Eva: I detracted the DNA from a banana once.

We reckoned Eva might give Jude a run for his money. Eva's mum describes her as, 'Clever, girly, funny, feisty, bossy.' And her dad adds, 'While she enjoys doing traditionally girly things, it's not what defines her. What defines Eva is that she can do anything. When she found out about Theresa May becoming prime minister, there were just a look in her eyes of sheer astonishment, and she were like, I could be prime minister.'

But teaching is a skill requiring quite complex cognitive processes and teaching a physical activity is particularly hard because you have to mirror your pupil's movements. It's very easy to confuse yourself and the other person. Eva wasn't fazed: 'Bend your leg at the front, yeah, that's it. This is your punching hand, so put it on your belt.' Jude immediately put it on his waist like a teapot and swayed his hips. 'No, on your belt,' she laughed, adding encouragingly, 'so, you're doing it quite right, but you just need to do ki-ai! Ki-ai!'

She's really impressive, and as Professor Howard-Jones points out, 'She's monitoring his performance and giving the instructions that are appropriate, and that sort of contingent teaching is unusual to see until children are about seven years old.'

Afterwards she gets the ultimate compliment from

Are the differences in the brain fixed?

Some studies have reported that boys are generally better than girls at imagining what objects look like when they are rotated – so-called mental rotation skills. However, training in these skills has been shown to improve them, to the extent that such training could reduce or even reverse the supposed sex difference. In studies with adults, being reminded of positive gender stereotypes has also been shown to improve abilities of women in the mental-rotation task, while negative stereotypes disrupted performance and the operation of brain circuits required for success. It certainly seems that our culture has a massive influence on how we experience sex differences, and that culture influences our brain development, behaviour and abilities.

Jude: 'Eva's been learning me how to do karate. She was very tough and very strong, like The Hulk.'

Eva and Jude's pairing was just one of many clear examples of boys and girls enjoying and benefiting from each other during the week they spent together, and it was heartening to see the strongly gendered cultures that had emerged in the same-sex week broken down in favour of a more fluid and inclusive environment for all.

The issue of gender is so complicated to unpick and such a minefield to explore that we were wary of venturing into it. However, the experiment with our five-year-olds gave us a little window onto the ways in which girls and boys behave, how they play, how they relate, how they interact.

Ultimately, across the series the differences we saw *between* the girls and boys were often smaller than the range and diversity of behaviour that we saw *within* groups of girls or boys. Just knowing whether someone is a boy or a girl is always going to be a poor predictor of his or her behaviour, ideas and attitudes.

That said, we did see marked differences in styles of

play, in language skills and acquisition, expressions of empathy, attitudes to risk, and in the kinds of group culture that emerged in each group, notwithstanding the exceptions like Alice.

Whether those differences were caused by nature and early brain development or by nurture, experience and social conditioning is a question at the cutting-edge of current scientific research, and a debate that will run and run. What we can say with certainty is that the role models that are all around us in the media and popular culture *are* often strongly gendered and that our five-year-olds had already absorbed some of these stereotypes.

In an era when some people still feel comfortable referring to 'boy jobs' and 'girl jobs', watching our children at this age feels especially instructive. The relish with which our five-year-olds moved away from stereotypical ideas of gender and embraced a more fluid attitude to what boys and girls could do and be has lessons for us all.

Let's hear it for make-up for boys, trucks for girls, and pink for all.

How important are sex and gender differences in the end?

Sex differences are an essential part of the evolutionary processes from which our species emerged. We can't buck them – we can only learn about them and try to interpret what they do and don't mean for us as individuals and as a society. However, what is very clear is that the two sexes are far more similar than different in their psychological abilities. So much so, in fact, that some scientists are now promoting a 'gender similarities hypothesis' rather than looking for differences. Sex differences and gender will remain a popular fascination and feed strongly into our individual sense of identity but, in reality, only a very small part of our potential will ever be explained by whether we are a girl or a boy.

A guide to . . . the difference between girls and boys

What can girls do that boys can't?

Siena: They can wear dresses.

Eva: Hey, boys can too.

Siena: No they can't.

Eva: Yes they can.

Siena: Wear lipstick.

Oliver: Some girls get their ears pierced and boys don't.

Eva: Boys can. My brother wears lipstick, lipstick [lipsalve] for school.

Harry: Boys don't wear tutus and girls do.

Oscar: Boys are stronger than girls. Well, girls can be strong, it's cos that they have to take lessons.

Jude R: Girls have long eyelashes.

Eva: Girls and boys are kind. Some girls are mean, some boys are mean. Boys aren't better than girls, they're exactly the same. They're exactly the same.

resisting
temptation

Zoë: Oh sweets! I can put so many in my mouth at the same time.

As we said at the beginning of this book, one of the great insights of the programme has been sneaking a peek at children as they're dealing with temptation, whether that's a chocolate cake, a chocolate fountain or an object of desire like balloons or a confetti machine. Without an adult there to set the parameters, their attitudes to temptation seem to tell us something fundamental about ourselves.

As well as making us laugh, seeing how the children react is also very revealing. Who pushes at the boundaries, who keeps well within them? Who polices the situation, and according to whose rules? We want children to follow certain rules – don't step in the road, don't touch the gas ring – so they will be safe. And we also want them to make good choices about doing the right thing. The Temptation Tasks showed us how we learn to interpret and implement the rules.

Elliot, did you tell Zoë to turn it?
Elliot: Yeah. But . . . she listened.

It is around this age that children are beginning to *internalize* rules and to develop a sense of self-control, so that they are not entirely impulse-driven. Tempting situations are as much a litmus test of their morality as their ability to defer gratification. And with the children in *The Secret Life of 4, 5 and 6 Year Olds* we got a wonderfully vivid sense of these children's moral compass when we put temptation in their way.

The Rigged Sweet Machine

Unlike your average gumball dispenser requiring coins in return for a handful of sweets, ours was specially rigged. If someone so much as gave the handle a quick try the sweets would keep coming until the machine was empty. How would our four-year-olds react?

After lunch, this shiny sweet machine appeared in the classroom; the four-year-olds were told that it was for later. The excitement was palpable and, with the teacher out of the room, the children started dancing around the machine, drooling and drumming it with their fingers, leaping up and down to see if they could accidentally set it off. One boy, Elliot, got very interested in the mechanics of how you could possibly get sweets without money. But remembering the instruction they didn't turn the handle . . . until a new girl called Zoë came in who hadn't been told that it was for later. Seizing the opportunity, Elliot said, casually, 'Do you want to turn it?' And she did. Joyous mayhem ensued. Some children sat and stuffed as many sweets in their mouths as they could, others were immediately concerned about the consequences and tried desperately to sweep up the sweets.

Catastrophe or great good fortune?
Compare the children's responses:

Charlotte: If [teacher] Kate comes back she will be so mad at us.

Charlotte: Nobody turn it any more, okay?

Tia: I just keep doing it by accident . . . !

When the teacher came back and asked them what happened Zoë owned up straight away, 'Yes I did turn it.' But then she turned to Elliot and said, 'He told me to do it.' Elliot was put on the spot but he gave as good as he got with his, 'Yeah, but she listened.'

At four years old their desires are paramount, but already their responses diverge wildly, some desperate to uphold law and order, others keen to make the best of the opportunity.

Kash: What about we say when we came in the classroom we were so shocked they were already on the floor?

How does this response compare with our six-year-olds? Same machine, same instruction, but if anything they turned the handle even quicker, so much so that in the melee that followed, it wasn't clear who actually did

Why do children find it so hard to resist a treat?

Young children can find it difficult to resist the treat in front of them, even when they've been promised they'll have two treats later as a reward. This is not a failure to calculate the benefits of holding on, but simply an inability to control the impulse to reach out.

Using neuroimaging, researchers have shown that the brains of young children in this situation are successfully evaluating the possible outcomes. In contrast, the brain region for controlling their automatic impulse is still very much a 'work in progress' and it's this part of the brain that's just not yet up to the task. As this part of the brain gradually develops, so children slowly improve their ability to resist temptation.

it. But the smart money was on Kash, who wasn't afraid to take risks and was the most resourceful when it came to making up a good story. In fact, they tripped off his tongue:

> Kash: I was running to it like this, yeah, and I accidentally fell and banged it.

But just as with the four-year-olds, one six-year-old, Elvin, stepped in even before the handle was turned, saying, 'Don't touch. It's for later.' And he was traumatized by the sight of the sweets cascading all over the floor and immediately started corralling the group into hiding the sweets in every teapot, saucepan and cupboard they could find. This seemed to be motivated entirely by his reading of the emotional consequences that might follow in the fallout from the situation: 'I'm going to be in trouble. My mum and dad will be so cross,' and worse still, 'Beatrice is going to be so mad at me and then she wouldn't want to be my friend again.' Elvin was outraged by Kash's willingness to tell fibs:

> Elvin: No! We have to tell the truth. If we tell a lie we'll be even in more trouble.

Elvin felt responsible for the fact that he had let people down, even though in fact it was anything but his responsibility, and he imagined the possible consequences in lurid detail and was upset by them. And as Dr Kilbey remarked, 'Teachers and parents will tell you that for some children you need to be volcanic in your expression to them – voice, face, body language. With Elvin, a very quiet "I'm quite disappointed in you" is going to have exactly the same effect.'

Again we saw two contrasting responses to temptation and broken rules, one catastrophic, one opportunistic. In the end Kash did admit that he was the one who turned it, but he was outraged at the suggestion that he did it on purpose:

> Kash: Why is everyone thinking that I did it on purpose? Who thinks I did it on purpose now? I swear on God's life and Jesus' life and God's mum's life . . .

But let's rewind and try and unpick the complicated mental processes that are kicking in here for Elvin, Kash, Charlotte, Zoë and Elliot.

Decision-making

Above all it is our self-control that enables us to set priorities and resist impulsive responses to temptation. As we saw with Charlotte, she was already able to exercise supreme self-control at just four years old.

It turns out that there are two other mental processes, or 'executive functions', that go into every choice or decision we make, including whether to resist a temptation, how to deal with the consequences and whether to own up. It is our 'working memory' that holds an instruction like 'it's for later' in our heads, and it's our 'mental flexibility' that allows us to see things from different perspectives and to learn from our mistakes. Confronted with 'the problem' of sweets strewn all over the floor, we saw very different levels of mental flexibility emerging – everything from blind panic to inventive crisis plans, which involved stuffing every crevice with the incriminating sweets.

How do we learn to be good?

Our sense of morality is about making judgements about the actions and intentions of others and ourselves, and it appears very tied up with our emotional processing in social situations. These 'social emotions' provide an important guide to us. Before one year old we can already respond to whether an adult is behaving in a helpful fashion to another. So, even before we have language, it seems we are beginning to make a judgement about what it means to be a helpful person, which will feed into our ideas about what it means to be 'good'. Our social emotions continue to feature in the moral decisions we make as adults, with our reasoning often having to 'catch up' after the decision has essentially been made. The reasoning is always important, however, not least because it helps us talk about the situation and develop rules together about how we should behave in the future.

But children aren't born with self-control and these other decision-making skills; they are born with the *potential* to develop them, and these skills are being honed around this time. That's the beauty of seeing them put to the test in our temptation tasks on *Secret Life*.

The rule makers

What is it that gives children as far apart in age as Charlotte and Elvin such a deep-seated sense of right and wrong? Whenever we saw this kind of morality at work in the children at the younger end of our age range it was riveting.

Four-year-old Enzo, whom we met giving the teachers a run for their money in 'Language and the art of persuasion', also had a strong moral compass.

When a group of the four-year-olds were challenged

A guide to . . . upholding the rules

Why d'you think we have rules?

Elvin: Because rules, they – they save lives.

Do you like following the rules?

Milana: I prefer to make the rules up myself.

What d'you think would happen if we had no rules?

Bea: Everything would start getting really crazy.

Teacher: Kash, did you eat a single sweet?

Kash: I swear on God's life and Jesus' life and God's mum's life . . . I just took one, that's it.

Caspar: No, he put loads in his mouth.

Teacher: So did you eat some sweets or did you not eat any sweets?

Kash: That is such a lie, I only ate one.

Teacher: Kash!

Kash: I ate three. Three. I just ate three, so am I allowed some more because I already, like, ate a little bit, like?

to sit in silence for ten long minutes with the reward of being allowed to play with an electronic megaphone left invitingly close by, it was agony for Enzo. Not only did he feel compelled to do as he'd been told, but the sight of other children having a sneaky go was torture to him. It was the double bind that they were breaking the rules *and* that he couldn't report them. By the end he was just bursting with indignation as he blurted out, 'Kate, the time has gone and do you know, while the timer's on, everyone spoke into it except for me. So I win it.'

Enzo's dad says that his brain never switches off and Mum adds that she thinks he's either going to be, 'An engineer . . . or a dictator.'

Sticking to the rules is very tricky in a group situation like the Megaphone Challenge and it's easy to forget – as several of the children do – that you have to take responsibility for yourself, even when the other children don't. But even harder to keep in your head is a set of rules whereby if one transgresses *everybody* loses out. This makes great demands on your working memory and raises the stakes considerably. And a simple test of resisting temptation becomes a social task instead – how well can a group of four-year-olds police itself?

The Golden Coins

These were the rules when Tia's class of four-year-olds were told that if they could all remain on their seats while the teacher went out of the room they would all get some chocolate coins. If anyone got up . . . no coins.

As with the megaphone, whether through mischief or memory lapse, two children were unable to resist getting up and were out of their seats before the door had closed on the teacher. One was Tia, and she pleaded with the group not to tell on her and Jack. She alone seemed to grasp that they had shared responsibility – if one person got in trouble, they would all be penalized – and suggested they cover up her mistake for the sake of the prize. But a law-abiding child like Charlotte could never fall in with this, and she told Tia she was going to tell the teacher simply because 'we can't win'. At this point it turned coercive and the exchange that followed gave us a brilliant insight into their moral landscape. Under duress Tia threatened, 'If you tell . . . I'll tell my mummy and daddy and my sister. My aunt Germaine and my . . . and my daddy. Also my grandad and my two nannies.'

At that Charlotte raised the stakes: 'And I'm going to tell Father Christmas and the Tooth Fairy.'

Unusually for Tia, she was lost for words. Tia and Charlotte referenced the most important moral authorities in their life, all 'people', as Professor Howard-Jones points out, who make judgements about the children's behaviour.

In Charlotte's moral universe it's not who knows about a transgression that counts, it's the fact that it happened, and intriguingly the moral authorities she calls on are all-seeing 'others', unlike Tia's who are real people in her family. But it is Charlotte's morality that wins out. The teacher is told and there are no chocolate coins for the four-year-olds that day.

The rule-breakers

But before we celebrate the wonder of self-control in such young children, let's spare a thought for the Lords and Ladies of Misrule and remember that not only is it enormous fun to break the rules, it can also be important sometimes, even a sign of intelligence.

As Professor Howard-Jones points out, 'There's a reason why naughtiness can be so enjoyable, and if

Cuba: Really if you feel my trumps I would blow this whole house down and that's why I'm trying not to trump.

you're always following the rules you don't experience that. It's important to be able to break the rules sometimes. It's quite difficult to ever do anything unique in life if you don't break conventions.'

To conclude, it does seem that self-control can be as present in a four-year-old as a six-year-old. Where do Enzo's, Charlotte's or Elvin's self-control and moral certainty come from? Is it from the way they are being raised and their social situations? Or is it predetermined, from their genes? Repeatedly through *The Secret Life of 4, 5 and 6 Year Olds* we came up against the nature–nurture debate, and we felt the latest thinking – that nature and nurture go to work upon each other in inextricable ways – was being played out in front of our eyes in the children's behaviour.

What is happening when we feel temptation?

The brain circuits used to evaluate different aspects of a situation are rapidly developing in young children. These circuits can also develop at different rates in the same individual. A reassuring sense of 'moral certainty' – when we feel sure what should be done – arises when our different circuits are guiding us in the same direction. However, particularly in a child, such a sense may also reflect one circuit just being better developed than the others, causing one simple aspect of the situation to dominate.

Children and adults often encounter moral dilemmas, such as when a sense of fairness conflicts with our love for friends or our more selfish desires. In these situations, the circuits needed to assess the situation may compete with each other, as they guide us in quite different directions. The resulting sense of 'mixed feelings' can be uncomfortable and confusing, but these dilemmas are an important spur for learning. They prompt us to develop our moral reasoning – as we try to balance different ways of looking at the same situation.

What would you do if you were queen?

> Elouisa: I would get some slaves and tell them to make me a cup of tea.

> Caitlyn: I would get everything that I want, I'd even get a flying unicorn.

Imagine, Elvin, if you were king for the day, what would you do?

> Elvin: I would say everyone you need to do what I say.

What kind of rules would you have?

> Marley: Never ever hit, erm, a teacher or adult, never ever let your dog off the leash . . . And never ever, ever, ever watch YouTube on the plane.

making your own rules

Caitlyn: Okay, so we need to make some rules about this club. You have to join today if you wanna be in the club. That's rule number one. If the head of the club – which is me – asks them to go to a meeting, they go to a meeting. Assistant Number One, I'll get the hideout ready and you tell everyone, 'If you want to join our club, join it today or never.' Okay?

What's the naughtiest thing somebody could do?

What do you like about Cuba?

Leila: Erm, steal a whole house.

Shakir: Good at not behaving. Wiggling his bum at the teacher. Eating his bogeys.

Skyla: You know that bully-boy, if he troubles you just bite him.

Aniyah: Okay. But I will get in trouble. He will tell me off.

Skyla: But my daddy said that so I'm going to do it.

learning to lie,
learning to love

What happened to the chocolate cake, boys?

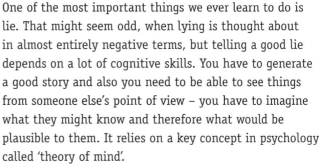

One of the most important things we ever learn to do is lie. That might seem odd, when lying is thought about in almost entirely negative terms, but telling a good lie depends on a lot of cognitive skills. You have to generate a good story and also you need to be able to see things from someone else's point of view – you have to imagine what they might know and therefore what would be plausible to them. It relies on a key concept in psychology called 'theory of mind'.

When you play Peekaboo with a child, they cover their face with their hands and can hardly contain their excitement as they wait for you to 'find' them. That's because they can't see you so they assume you can't see them either, a neat demonstration of the fact that we aren't born with the ability to understand that other people have minds, or their own point of view. It's something we have to learn.

Theory of mind doesn't kick in until the age of about four, and there are countless examples of the difference it makes throughout *The Secret Life of 4, 5 and 6 Year Olds*.

When we do Show and Tell with the four-year-old children they look at the object or book they've brought in without realizing they need to turn it around so the rest of the group can see it too. They still think the whole group shares their point of view. By six they understand that other people have a different perspective. They hold up their toy and ask, 'Can you all see?' They move around to show it to different people, understanding that each of them has a different view of the same situation.

And it isn't until you have a solid grasp of theory of mind that you can tell a big fat whopper. The moments when our children's ability to lie is tested have become some of the most loved in the show.

We need to talk about chocolate

This new skill of lying was brilliantly explored in our test The Unmanned Chocolate Cake, in which a cake was left unsupervised with no instructions near the children. Chocolate is pretty irresistible to a child and it was unlikely they would be able to refrain from a quick taste. How did our four, five and six-year-olds respond, and crucially what did they say if the cake showed evidence of being tampered with?

The four-year-olds

When we did the test with the four-year-olds, one boy, Chaim, dived straight in. He saw it as fair game – after all there was nothing to say he shouldn't – and he wasn't afraid of the consequences. There's something refreshingly straightforward about his 'There's a big chocolate cake and I'm going to eat it', and the scientists are quick to point out that this kind of curiosity and pushing at boundaries can be a sign of intelligence. Chaim persuades Christian to dip his finger in too. What's important here is what happened next; when the teacher returned and asked whether anyone had touched the cake, Chaim owned up straight away:

Boys, has anyone eaten some of my cake? Chaim: I have.

Christian's impulse was also to tell the truth, as if the teacher would somehow know if he hadn't. 'It got on my hands. I put it in my mouth. I did that to get the chocolate off my hands.' They happened to have chocolate all over their faces too, which would have

Why is chocolate so tempting?

The distinctive smell of chocolate is one of its most alluring features and smell is key when it comes to triggering our memories, often evoking the first time we ever encountered the scent. Smell forms emotional memories in a unique way too, easily becoming associated with the pleasure (or pain) associated with the first encounter. Scientists believe a special smell network in our brain includes regions that also serve our emotions and memory, making it an important 'sense of first impressions' that can cause our memories to come flooding back.

been a giveaway, but this aside they didn't yet have the ability to problem-solve their way out of a pickle by inventing a convincing fib.

The five-year-olds

By the time the children had got to five it was a much more complicated affair.

One beautiful midsummer afternoon, we left a similar chocolate cake unattended in the playground. Two boys playing nearby, Alfie and Arthur, soon found it. Leaning over it, they exclaimed, 'It smells so chocolatey!'

As we discovered earlier, Alfie was seldom apart from Emily, but on this occasion he was playing with the boys. Alfie lives in Somerset with his mum and dad and baby sister, and he too has a tremendous natural sense of

George: A bird and a mini-beast . . .
Alfie: . . . flew down, ate it, and then flew back.

curiosity about the world. As he leant his nose as close as could be to the icing of the cake, it suddenly poked in and made a dent. With that, an invisible barrier was down and he went in for a lick, only to be joined by Arthur, and soon they were all at it, licking and poking and tasting the cake.

Suddenly the teacher appeared. 'Boys, can you all come here? I left this cake here a minute ago and when I've come back there seems to be lots of little bits missing, and lots of smudges everywhere.'

Arthur: It was someone mysterious did that big one.

Arthur: I don't know. We didn't see.

Teacher: Someone mysterious? What did they look like?

Charlie G, it seems, did see the mysterious creature because at this point he acts out a figure creeping around the cake. Meanwhile, George takes up the story and together they paint a scene of a pterodactyl-like bird, a mysterious creature and a plague of mini-beasts descending on the cake and laying waste to it.

In backing up each other's story and embellishing it, they colluded in making the lie much more persuasive. The teacher goes to get a knife so they can clear up the mess they've made. 'Once the boys have reached a state of shared responsibility,' Dr Wass points out, 'it becomes much easier for them to break the rules still further.' With the teacher out of sight again it was open season, and while the boys set about supposedly patching it up with a knife, the cake was more or less demolished.

George, five: No, no no. Don't just eat random bits. This is really serious. Oh . . . this bit is really smudged so I'll just eat it.

The six-year-olds

When it came to the six-year-olds, they were also left with a delicious-looking cake, this time decorated with mini cupcakes. They also dipped their fingers in the icing and ate some cake. And like the fives they lied to cover their tracks. But this time they rooted their lie very plausibly in the real world.

And because their theory of mind has had another year to develop, they were confident in their ability to lie convincingly. So now they played around with various outcomes, using their newfound skill to build allegiances and friendships. It was Leila who ate some cake. She told Caitlyn she'd done this. Caitlyn immediately threatened to tell the teacher, prompting Leila to retaliate with, 'I'll tell that *you* ate it.' Both Leila and Caitlyn understand that the teacher will at least entertain this lie, prompting Caitlyn to withdraw her threat: 'I was only joking.' Now they were in it together, whether they liked it or not, and when the teacher came back the girls collaborated and told a convincing lie, and they got off scot-free:

Caitlynn: Maybe the cupcake [icing] did fall off on the floor and then someone did accidentally step on it and that cupcake did stay on their trainer.

As the scientists remark, how ironic for parents that at the point their children learn to lie they can celebrate it as a huge developmental leap.

A guide to . . . chocolate

Chaim: Do you know there's a big chocolate cake? I'm going to eat it.

Luke: Don't you dare . . .

Chaim: What?

Luke: Don't eat it.

Chaim: Yummy!

George: This is really serious. Oh, this bit is off so I'll eat it.

Leila: What I want to do is eat the whole cake.

Arthur: Smell the cake, smell the cake.

Harry: I just really like chocolate.

Alfie: This makes my mouth water.

Elijah: Is that yummy?

Arthur: It smells chocolatey.

Harry: Yeah. Don't tell me off.

Alfie: Shall we lick the top?

George: No, no, no. No we can't do it cos we're kids. Don't just eat random bits.

Recognizing emotion

Developing a theory of mind doesn't happen all in one go or along a straight path, but an important first step is recognizing other people's emotions and feeling empathy. And the most common thing for children to notice is that someone else is distressed.

When four-year-old Tia saw a boy coming to the playroom for the first time, clutching a kangaroo and clinging to his dad and not wanting to come in by himself, she understood that he was in distress and instinctively she wanted to reach out to him. But she was inside on a chair and he was by the door, so she did the next best thing and put her arm around the boy sitting next to her and gave him a squeeze instead. He was surprised but pleased, Tia felt satisfied, and the new

Lola, four: Connie, now you just feel like me when I was sad.

What is theory of mind?

When we observe the actions of another, neurons in our brain fire as if we ourselves were performing the action. The firing of this 'mirror neuron system' can result in us unconsciously imitating the other person's actions. The brain circuitry of the mirror neuron system develops very early and this system can help us understand what others are doing and why. In other words, they can support a primitive theory of mind. For example, imagine a three-year-old who sees their friend hold out their hand to catch raindrops. As they automatically find themselves holding out their own hand, like they would when they catch a ball, it becomes easier to grasp that their friend thinks something is about to be caught.

False beliefs and false stories

A more conscious and intentional understanding of another's mind requires a quite different set of brain networks to mature. The development of these networks allows children to imagine consciously or 'mentalize' about the behaviour of others. By five years old these networks are helping a child predict what their friend will do based on a grasp of their friend's belief, even when their friend's belief is clearly false. This more advanced theory of mind also means children begin to appreciate some advantages in not telling the truth, and that a good 'cover story' can prevent someone blaming you, even though the story itself is false.

boy gingerly made his way to his seat unaware of this silent, empathetic gesture from one of his new classmates.

And when four-year-old playmates Lola and Connie had a falling out, and Connie was in tears and said to Lola, 'I want you to be my friend and play with me again,' Lola reads the cues – the facial expression and the tears – and she told her, empathetically, that she knew how that felt.

The trouble is Lola doesn't know what to do about it. So she goes and sits in another part of the playground and plays with a piece of grass. It doesn't look very thoughtful or kind, but at four years old Lola didn't yet know what to do with the information that Connie was unhappy or how to make Connie feel better. The next stage of theory of mind is predicting what you could do that would make someone feel better and this usually develops a bit later.

Knowing what to do about it

It was particularly moving watching the children developing their range of tools and strategies for supporting other people in distress. Their ability to imagine what it feels like

151

What are the two kinds of empathy?

Scientists distinguish between two types of empathy. 'Cognitive empathy' is more about our ability to mentally understand and think about the emotional reactions and perspectives of others and being able to recognize an emotion from someone's expression. It is more about mentalizing and theory of mind. 'Affective empathy' is more about our tendency to feel someone else's emotions and do something about them. This can be a more automatic response and it has also been studied in animals.

People with autistic spectrum disorder tend to have lower cognitive empathy. They can sometimes struggle to identify the desires and emotional states of those around them, but their affective empathy can be well within the normal range. In contrast, those with psychopathic tendencies tend to have impairments in their affective but not cognitive empathy. Their ability to understand and think about emotions is intact, but they struggle to feel what others feel and to care about it.

George: I have no one to play with.

Ruth: I'll play with you because no one wants to play with me either.

Ruth: What do you want me to draw next?

(George hands Ruth a blue pen)

Ruth: Yeah, blue's my favourite colour. Is it yours?

George: Yeah.

Ruth: You're really helpful.

to be someone else and to consider what might help them in a similar situation had begun to take root. Take five-year-olds Ruth and George. George is sad because no one wants to play with him. But Ruth sits down next to him and starts drawing, immediately putting George at ease:

Ruth uses all of her empathetic skills – she asks him questions, she compliments him, she encourages him – slowly drawing him back into social interaction:

George: Do you want me to draw a big heart for you?

Ruth: Yeah.

George: (Draws) Heart and star . . .

This shows the ability to recognize his feelings *and* to make him feel better, and slowly but surely George is drawn back into the room and engaged in two-way conversation in which he begins to ask questions, and this cements their friendship:

George: Which country are you from?

Ruth: I'm from Africa.

George: What part of Africa do you live in? Cos I went there before.

Ruth: Well I live in Ghana.

This ability to see someone in their entirety as someone separate to you, with their own thoughts and feelings, and yet wanting to reach out to them and support them, is the beginning of all deep attachment and, ultimately, of love.

George: I live in Hornchurch.

153

Can we really feel someone else's pain?

When we are close to someone we often say we can 'feel their pain', and recently scientists managed to demonstrate just how true that is. They studied the brain scans of people under threat of receiving small electrical shocks to either themselves, a friend or a stranger. When the person being threatened was a friend, the brain patterns were remarkably similar to those when the participants themselves were under threat. This overlap of 'self' and 'friend' in the brain may form an important basis for altruism. Friendship encourages us to expand the more selfish desires we feel for ourselves, until they include the selfless well-being of others.

By age six most of the children seemed to have reached a place where they could think, 'I really care enough about this other person to want them to be happy'. Their friends' emotions and states of mind were important to them and they wanted to offer support where they could. And this was in line with the predictions of our scientists, that by six most children would have developed both strands of empathy – both the recognizing and the doing something about it kind.

But as ever on *Secret Life* it's the exception proves the rule, and we met some four-year-olds who showed the most extraordinary empathy at a young age – both the ability to *imagine* someone else's thoughts and feelings and the desire to *respond* with an appropriate emotion or gesture.

When four-year-old Jayda was teaching Jessica a song and she saw that Jessica felt awkward and embarrassed in case she got it wrong, Jayda started coaching her:

Jayda: You have to do a big loud voice like this. Watch me. Now you try. Come on, come on, big loud voice.

Jessica: I can't.

Having first given her an example to follow Jayda read the signs and acknowledged the nerves:

> Jayda: You're a bit too shy.

Last of all she coaxed her:

> Jayda: Let's try one more try . . . Sing with me. Copy me. Copy the words what I'm saying, okay?

That offer to accompany someone on a difficult task, to do it alongside them, is as kind, thoughtful and supportive in a child as it would be in an adult. At four years old it was exceptional.

And very occasionally we were privileged to witness a moment when a child appeared to read someone else's emotions correctly for the very first time. When five-year-old Alfie was asked to paint a portrait of his classmate Ruth it was a big challenge for him. According to his mum, he had never done any painting at home and also he wasn't always able to interpret other people's feelings very accurately. As his dad put it, 'He does care about people but sometimes in the moment there's something else he cares about a bit more.'

At first Alfie didn't understand how much Ruth was invested in the image of her that he was painting. She wanted to see what colour he would use for her skin – she was Ghanaian – how he would represent her eyes, her hair, her mouth. When she told him she didn't like his picture and that he'd 'messed it up' and hadn't painted her face right, time stood still for Alfie and he almost lost heart.

'This is the most painful and difficult thing that children of this age have to do,' comments Dr Kilbey. 'When you stop being quite so obsessed with yourself and start tuning in to the thoughts and feelings and needs of others, you realize that you're getting it wrong. Imagine that moment of self-awareness – who wants to charge full on into *that*?'

Alfie is no quitter and he persevered until the Show and Tell with the teacher, and the scientists applauded him for his resilience. And when the children were asked to vote for the painting they liked the best, he read Ruth's emotions absolutely correctly, explaining to the teacher that she didn't like his picture but she didn't want to hurt his feelings and that's why she was hiding her face behind her painting. 'If you could watch development go in stages,' says Dr Kilbey, 'this is the halleluiah moment for Alfie, because he has had a window into Ruth's mind –

Why do you like looking after people?
Ellie-Mae: Because when you've got happy you're glad to share with everyone so they can be happy, then the others can be happy by passing on to each other.

> **Can we improve our understanding of what's in other people's minds?**
>
> Our ability to understand the minds of others and to empathize with them depends on our development and our learning. Many scientists now believe that even our mirror neuron system must be programmed by experiences that begin soon after birth. In other words, it depends on learning. Also, we cannot even begin to use our brain circuits for mentalizing unless we can pause sufficiently to consider the thoughts and feelings of others. For that reason, successful attempts to encourage greater empathy have often focused on self-control and learning to 'stop and think'. Our theory of mind helps us learn many things about others, but the evidence suggests our theory of mind depends on many skills that must first be learnt.

into her motives, thoughts and feelings – and said, "I get why she's upset."'

And as if that wasn't enough developmental learning for one morning, *he* was the one who comforted Ruth as she was crying, showing that as well as recognizing her emotions he knew what to do about them too.

From lying to love

Watching the children, we can't help remembering that learning empathy doesn't happen overnight. We learn it incrementally, often taking baby steps, and some of them backwards, but – taken together – these small steps make up a quantum leap in understanding. Unexpectedly, a journey that starts with learning to lie leads us inexorably towards the ability to experience compassion and ultimately to love and care for our fellow human beings. This is a journey that it never hurts us to be reminded of; even as adults we can forget just how key this is in our relationships with others.

A guide to . . . lying

Is Tia a good big sister?

Caspar: My dad wears high heels.

Amelia-Rose: No!

Tia: She said 'Yes'.

Taysia: (To her classmates) Are you four?

Milana: Yeah.

Taysia: Are you four?

Kahana: Yeah.

Kash: You know I'm actually from India.

Taysia: Are you four?

Sam: I am ten years old.

Elvin: Oh, so how do you speak in India?

Kash: I'm just kidding, I'm not from India.

Caspar: My granny is about a thousand now.

Caspar: My grandad is a hundred of course.

A guide to . . . love and caring

Try and take people's minds off it

(Connie looks sad) Taylor: Hi. What's wrong? I will help ya.

(Connie cries) Taylor: I know, you've got to try and cheer me up then I won't miss my family.

Lola: May I speak a minute with Elliot?

Teacher: Of course you can. I'll leave you to it.

Lola: Elliot. Elliot we need you. We're doing a quiz and you're going to really enjoy it.

Elliot: (Crying) No I'm not.

Lola: Come on Elliot . . .

Lola: (Gets up) Okay, you can just sit there.

Tell people exactly why you're upset

Leila: Why are you sad?

Caitlyn: Cos I did miss my monkeys.

Leila: Are you also sad because you have no one to play with?

Caitlyn: No, it's cos there are no more Hula Hoops.

Always give support . . . until you can't be bothered

Teacher: What can you do to help Ruth?

Alfie: I don't know. I just want her to hurry up and stop crying so we can carry on playing . . .

A guide to . . .

Keep a sense of perspective

Evie-Rae: It's dead. Does that mean we'll never be able to see it again?

Enzo: This is the worst day of our lives.

Enzo: The chick died in its shell. That's sad, innit?

Evie-Rae: So sad. (Teacher enters) Ooh, you smell nice.

Teacher: What do you think we should do?

Orlagh: Turn it into chicken nuggets.

life and death

Teacher: What shall we do then?

Orlagh: Have a funeral.

Taysia: It's really sad, isn't it?

Enzo: It's a good thing we're going to give it a nice little home. Bye bye chick.

Enzo: My gran and granpa are pretty old so soon they might die.

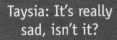

What's a funeral?

Maimoona: A funeral is whenever you go to Legoland.

how to win at
winning and losing

Charlie M: It's not about winning . . . when you're little . . . because when you're big you need to win.

The Secret Life of 4, 5 and 6 Year Olds embraces the view that team games and competitions offer the opportunity to develop a whole range of skills that can help us in our everyday lives – everything from how to work well in a team, to resilience and leadership, to respect for other people, empathy, and humility in handling success and failure. Best of all, the children learn from each other how to be a generous winner and a gracious loser.

This is not uncontroversial, and the debate around the pros and cons of competition and competitive sport in schools continues to rage. But we wanted to give the *Secret Life* children the experience of winning and losing, and we had confidence that this would uncover qualities that even they didn't know they possessed and reveal sides to their character that we hadn't seen.

Throughout our lives we win some, we lose some, and developing tools and coping strategies at this age is going

Which is more important, winning or having friends?

Phoenix: Having friends.

And why is that?

Phoenix: Because if you didn't have any friends then you wouldn't have anybody to play with.

What happens in the brain when we win?

When we win a competitive game we experience a surge in levels of the hormone testosterone. This temporarily loosens the connections between the cortex that leads our reasoning and those brain regions beneath our cortex that drive our impulses. The result can be a short-term increase in our impulsivity, aggression and dominance. The burst of testosterone that follows victory helps explain why those 'in the moment' celebrations in sport can resemble the dominance displays of other primates. In evolutionary terms, these behaviours probably helped us hang on to the spoils of victory when most of our energies had been spent gaining them. In a game, however, they have the potential to jeopardize valuable friendships. Generally, children have developed an ability to control their impulses by five to six years old, but mastery of their impulses in these 'hot' situations can take longer to develop.

to help immeasurably later on. As Dr Kilbey puts it, 'Team competition is really important at this age because they've mastered how to manage themselves individually, what they really need to work on is how they operate in a group; how you get along with other people, how you manage conflict, how you communicate. And this is what gets tapped into when you do a team activity.'

What makes a good friend when we lose?

One week we put on a kind of supersized sports day for our five-year-olds and played a series of team games; everything from a Football Tournament to a Fear Factor Challenge to a Cake Decorating Competition. And during the course of these games two five-year-olds

struck up a firm friendship, even though they often found themselves on opposite teams; tomboy Jet and Nat, our redhead from Wales.

Nat was a great competitor, throwing himself into each new game with enthusiasm, but he found himself on an unlucky losing streak. He just missed out at Musical Statues, he was reluctant to do the Fear Factor Challenge and he took his team to a photo finish in a very difficult task that involved crossing the playground using only two crates and a plank, losing out by a few seconds in a challenge lasting nearly fifteen minutes. 'What do *we* get?' he asked when the winning team was announced. After this he took himself off to a quiet spot on his own to lick his wounds, but we were immensely touched as he began to sing to himself, falteringly at first but soon with a strong pure voice, a solo from *Annie*. And that done, he went back to play with the others.

Finally, as captain of the boys' football team, we watched him step up and show incredible team leadership and a masterful ability to handle competing egos on his team (he offered Jude 'the second captaincy' which sounded much better than any alternative). He took the boys to a two-goal lead, and we could feel his hands on the trophy, only for the girls to draw level. Then – in a nail-biting finish – his best friend and super-striker, Jet, the captain of the girls, nicked a winning goal and the trophy was theirs.

Sometimes life is just not fair.

Nat: You got the trophy and I really wanted the trophy. Jet: I know, but . . . you should've tried harder.

Nat was crushed. He had done everything right and he still hadn't won. We didn't know how he would pick himself up after this or what it would mean for Nat and Jet's friendship. Until then Jet had thrown herself into every challenge with what looked like the simple love of competing, taking the winning or the losing in her stride. Would she understand the depth of Nat's feelings? Initially she seemed surprised to see him so upset by his team's defeat:

Jet: That was awesome. (Pause) Why are you sad? Why are you sad?

Nat: Cos you got the trophy and I really wanted the trophy.

Jet: I know, but . . . you should've tried harder.

Jet: Maybe next time . . .

Nat: I was!

Nat: I really have never had one.

Jet is refreshingly straightforward and so is he, owning up to his trophy-envy in a way that helps her to gauge his feelings accurately. We can see how deep he has to dig, but his inner resources took us all by surprise:

Jet: Maybe you can play again . . .

Jet: What's your plan?

Nat: No, no . . . I don't need it. I've already got a plan.

Nat: To get a football champion to teach me.

It's an object lesson in how to be generous in victory and gracious in defeat. Jet acknowledges Nat's disappointment and she gives him the space to come up with his own solution. He engages his imagination and finds solace in a fantasy scenario, just plausible enough

Why does losing feel so bad?

Scientists usually expect to see a drop in testosterone levels after losing, but this doesn't always happen and some studies have even shown a rise. It seems a number of factors influence the emotional and hormonal response to winning and losing and one of these is personality. Personalities that have an implicit need for power and dominance appear to be affected more by competition. Among these individuals, winning is more likely to elevate testosterone and losing is more likely to produce an increase in the stress hormone cortisol.

to comfort him. He even has a pragmatic fall-back plan, which is to nick one of his brother's trophies as he's got two. The passions aroused by the beautiful game have brought out the best in both of them.

As Dr Kilbey comments, 'Actually sometimes I think we need to *not* protect children quite so much, not to worry quite so much about what these experiences do to them, because they have their own cognitions and their own ways of working through them. They are very resilient in that way, and winning and losing allows that to flourish.'

Why do you like to win at things?
Nat: So more people like me.

Why does someone else losing feel so good?

When scoring points in a competitive game, anticipation of increasing our score activates reward regions beneath our cortex (involved with our motivation). Watching our competitor about to lose points produces a similar response in these regions of our brain to when we are about to win some.

Elvin: We win. We win. You lose. You lose. We win. We're the winners. You lost. They lost! Yeah, they lost. Losers . . .

The winner is . . . Team Fire Bum

We saw an awful lot of victory celebrations on *The Secret Life of 4, 5 and 6 Year Olds*. Let's compare this, and competition generally, across the four, five and six-year-olds.

When it comes to competition, the challenge for our four-year-olds is less about learning how to win and lose and more about learning to compete; understanding and retaining the rules of the game, especially if there is more than one, is still an effort for some of them. A game that is simple to us – I put the beanbag on my head, I don't touch it, I walk to the other side of the playground, trying to keep it on my head – can be a challenge for them.

That said, in the case of this relay race the girls had no problems following the instructions while the boys took a looser approach and circumnavigated the rules.

But in general you can see the four-year-olds are still on the threshold of a social world in which they will learn to follow rules and instructions and play ever more complex games. And, with some notable exceptions, their response to winning and losing is delightfully unregulated; they don't hide their palpable excitement, they taunt the losers and they celebrate their victories with exuberance. But these heightened emotions quickly pass.

Our four-year-olds are nothing if not reliably inconsistent. A pattern emerged – a child self-regulates beautifully one day, consoling her fellow losers, and the

next day she rubs defeat in the nose of her opponents, doing the very thing that upset her the day before. One step forward, two steps back.

You might expect to see more self-regulation one year on in the five-year-olds, but if anything the agony and the ecstasy of winning and losing are etched even more vividly across their faces. Perhaps that year at school has given them a clearer sense of what it means to compete as a team, and we see how much sport and competition mean to them – they seem to invest their whole being in the game and they *really* care about the outcome.

As a result we saw *less* regulation; abject despair at being called out, rage at a friend beating you to the prize, victory celebrations as glorious as they were ungracious. My favourite from a boy who named his team Fire Bum Bum. On hearing they'd won, he jumped on a chair and waved his backside at the assembled party shouting, 'My bum bum's happy. Bum bum, you're happy, bum bum.' And when asked to stop couldn't resist giving one last wiggle, one last shake of his victorious 'bum bum'.

Do you know what competitive means? Bea: Competitive means you want to win always.

By six years old we see a more pragmatic approach emerging in some of the children, and an impressive ability to talk themselves down. When Beatrice loses a Tug of War her friend Elouisa reminds her, with touching empathy, that in the Olympics they have three medallists not just one. And Bea herself chokes back tears as she consoles herself with the thought that they'll probably win next time because she will try harder.

But old habits die hard, especially when tensions run high. In striking contrast to the four-year-olds, who live in the moment and have an enviable ability to move on and forget the highs and lows, our six-year-olds bear grudges and they take time to recover from knocks and defeats as their emotional landscape becomes more layered and complex. As we saw in the chapter 'Feelings and what to do with them', when Beatrice befriends Elouisa over old friend Elvin, he can't jump up quick enough and do a victory dance right in her face when his team beats hers. The win is invested with emotional weight, and this is his chance to get his own back. Of course it doesn't end well for him – Beatrice takes a poor view of that kind of bragging – and he has some repairing to do before they can get back on track.

Bea: Maybe he was just celebrating but sometimes celebrating can hurt someone's feelings.

What would you like your team to be called?

Lola: Team Friendship.

Theo: Team Rainbow Coloured of Golden Sun.

Chaim: Mind Breakers.

George: Storm Creative.

Charlotte: The Quizzy Whizzy Team.

Ruth: Team Rose.

What is two plus three?

Team Friendship: Seventy?

Team Rainbow: Erm, we think five.

How many healthy foods can you name?

Team Rainbow: Apple, cheese, cauliflower and broccoli and carrots and fish and apples.

Team Friendship: Broccoli and carrots and cheese pasta and . . . toast . . . chocolate spread.

How many days are there in a week?

Team Friendship: Seventeen?

Team Rainbow: Five . . . no, seven I think.

winning at quizzes

What is the fastest animal in the world?

Storm Creative: Lion.

Team Rose: Cheetah.

What is the biggest number?

George: One hundred and one.

Alfie for Team Rose: Nine zillion and ninety-nine.

George: Infinity.

Why does it rain?

Storm Creative: Stormy clouds and water cycles and lightning.

Team Rose: Erm, so that the flowers can get some water.

Which is bigger, London or England?

Team Storm: London.

Team Rose: London.

Why does winning and losing affect boys and girls so differently?

Competition creates heated moments in which we release hormones that impact on how our brain functions. Genetics have a big role to play in this process and in explaining why one person responds so differently to another, but the picture is made complicated by many factors, including whether the individual concerned is male or female.

Scientists have identified several specific genes that influence the release of hormones in competitive situations, but these genes appear to affect males and females differently. For example, one of these genes is linked to more testosterone among males, but not among females. This may explain why we see more evidence for bursts of testosterone among victorious men than victorious women and why boys appear more prone to victory displays than girls. Our response to losing is not all about our genes. With experience, we can learn to look at things in ways that lessen the sting. One common strategy is to put losing down to bad luck rather than personal performance. Acquiring the skills to make helpful 'alternative constructions' is all part of learning to regulate our emotions.

Nat wins the Golden Spoon

As a postscript I should mention that Nat did win a trophy that week; on the last day he took home the Golden Spoon for the Best Cake Decoration, and in a touching bookend to the football match, Jet – on the opposing team again – came right up and congratulated Nat and his partner on their win, 'You have a trophy. Well done Nat and well done Calla.'

Winning and losing and the school of hard knocks is not to everyone's taste, and it can be painful to watch a child lose and to see fierce competitiveness in one's own children. But on the programme we saw evidence of children growing immeasurably through competitive

Jet: We just play fun – it's just a game. It's just a game.

situations, coming to terms with both winning and losing, and above all harnessing skills of determination and empathy and resilience that even they didn't know they possessed.

In competitive games, as in any competitive situation in life, the pressures are part extrinsic – the rules of the game – and part intrinsic – what we bring of *ourselves* to any competitive situation. We can all invest challenges with additional difficulty and complexity as some of the children did. Or we can take a leaf out of Jet's book and approach competition with genuine appetite and desire, but treat the outcome with composure, and be as gracious in victory as we are in defeat.

Is competition good for us?

Competition usually involves 'hot' moments and periods of excitement when hormones are impacting on our thinking processes. Acting on impulse during these moments can sometimes benefit our social standing and happiness but it can also threaten them – including in ways that extend beyond the game itself. It generally helps in life if you can reason about a situation before you act – even in the heat of the moment – and every competition is an opportunity to practise the skills required. For example, if the emotional content is difficult, you can learn to conjure up ideas that diminish their impact, for example 'it's only a game'. Competitive games can encourage children to nurture the emotional regulation they need for momentary reflection in 'hot' situations. In these and many other ways, competitive games can be a boon for children's learning and development.

Share your winnings with the losers

Remind your twin that blood is thicker than water

Alice: Do you want to share? You can have a heart, I can have a heart.

Samuel: Brother, I was going to win. Can I have your crown?

Oliver: We will share the crown.

Siena: You're really nice, aren't you?

Siena: I don't usually play with Alice but when she gave me the sweets, we became good friends.

Phoenix: Jude, the next time I win a game I'll give the prize to you.

Offer to win for your friend next time

Phoenix: Yeah.

Jude: The whole prize?

Jude: Thank you. Try and do your best so you can win the bags to give to me.

winning graciously

Don't gloat

Jack: (Running around the playground shouting) We beat you girls. Woo! I'm gonna win, I'm gonna win.

Don't wave your bum in your opponent's face

Elijah: My bum bum's happy. Bum bum, you're happy.

Don't perform an impromptu victory rap dance to the losers

Elvin and Poppy: We win. We win. You lose. You lose. We win. We're the winners. You lost. They lost! Yeah, they lost. Losers . . .

A guide to . . .

Comfort your fellow losers and congratulate the winners

Tia: We tried our best but we just lost. I'm so glad you won.

Congragnations! Hi five, Joe!

Talk yourself down

Bea: Don't worry, I think we'll win next time.

Don't break the winning entry

Tyreece: We broke their tower. It was really funny. It was a joke.

losing graciously

Don't steal back the prize
after losing the race

Jude: Can you go and get
Phoenix's chocolate for us?
Say 'Phoenix look, there's an
elephant behind you' and then
you snatch it. Go!

Don't punish the winner

Jaja: You had the
medal and it's not fair
to me! So you can't join
in my game . . .

Don't squash ladybirds

Kahana: Look, a
Ladybird. (Squashes it)
And now I happy.

if at first you don't succeed . . .

Across all the episodes we made, there was one quality that stood out above all else when we saw it on the programme, and not just in competitions. Time and again on *The Secret Life of 4, 5 and 6 Year Olds* there were children who impressed us in a way that was both hard to put your finger on and blindingly obvious; simply put, when the going got tough they didn't give up.

Christian: There, it's perfect!

These children had the ability to stick at something, however frustrating or difficult, until it was done. Some were rewarded for their efforts, others weren't, but in each case we saw these children grow in self-confidence as they persevered, overcame their difficulties and moved on to something new. And the really interesting thing was seeing how they carried this increased self-esteem with them and on to the next challenge.

Take Christian, for example.

We first met him when he was four years old and we noticed straight away how well turned out he was. His mum described him as 'particular': 'He can't just wear any old shirt, it's got to be a particular shirt. The trousers have to sit just right on top of the shoes, it has to be just right. He's very much a right and wrong person.'

'Done any den building?' asked teacher Kate one morning. 'Because today, we're going to be builders.' Two teams were chosen with the less dominant children on one side and the more dominant children on the other.

A recipe for disaster? As the less dominant team started collaborating, the dominant characters were immediately at odds. One girl said, 'It's gonna be the wildest house I ever made.' A fight broke out over a plank . . . and Christian, who was trying his best to corral the troops, said, 'This is why we need to work together.' They failed spectacularly to get their house off the ground, let alone decorated, and Christian told teacher Kate that he was sad.

Then something remarkable happened. After the other team had won the prize, Christian went back to his team's den and set to work finishing it off; he asked the others to help him, 'Do you want to help me finish off the hideout?' But when none of them did he didn't give up. Single-handedly he painstakingly sawed the cardboard and taped it together to make the door. He retreated inside and finished the windows. When his work was done, he pulled the two cardboard doors towards him until all we could see was a beady eye gleaming in the dark.

'Looks good to me,' he said, as he closed the doors all the way. And we heard a small voice say under his breath, 'It's perfect.'

During this time we got a message that one of the mums was concerned about her son. The parents were watching on monitors in another room as the children built their dens and, after Christian's team lost, his mum lost sight of him, and she was worried he might be on his own somewhere, upset about losing.

Our production room was right next to the playground and I brought her in so she could see what was happening on the other side of the long window. The scientists were so excited by Christian's efforts that they had left their monitors and were also looking directly out of the window at this small boy determinedly wrestling a piece of cardboard into submission. Dr Wass complimented his mum on her son's phenomenal staying power. And his mum welled up. In the programme Dr Wass explained, 'This is a personality attribute that's much studied by psychologists, it's called grit and determination, and it's something Christian's got in spades.'

Long-term and short-term goals – what's the difference in our brain?

We use our cortex to imagine long-term goals, but these goals don't always get us excited like short-term ones. For example, when we see a piece of chocolate cake in front of us, most of us feel quite motivated to grab some short-term satisfaction. That motivation is related to the reward regions beneath our cortex increasing their activation. Those of us with more grit have more of a connection between the cortex we use for thinking about our long-term goals and the reward circuitry that lies beneath it. This helps our future goals to stimulate the persistent sense of motivation required to achieve them.

What's a growth mindset?

While we were looking into the science behind *Secret Life*, we came across the American researcher Professor Carol Dweck, who has done fascinating research in this area, specifically on the effect of praise on children's self-esteem. She and her team took 400 children aged ten and eleven and gave them a simple IQ test. At the end of the test they praised all the pupils in one of two ways: half were praised for their intelligence – 'you must be really clever at these tests' – and the other half were praised for their effort – 'you must have worked really hard at that'. A subtle difference, but the impact proved to be huge.

Now *all* the children had to do another test but they were offered a choice; they could do a harder version, with an opportunity to learn, or an easy version, one they would definitely be good at. Of the children praised for their innate intelligence, 67 per cent chose the easy test, while of the children praised for effort, an incredible 92 per cent chose the hard test.

Professor Dweck thinks this has lessons for all of us. Her view is that the child or adult who is praised for their intelligence hears that they are being praised for being brilliant and talented, and think that's why they're being admired and valued. So they try not to do anything that will disprove that evaluation. As a result, they enter what Dweck calls a 'fixed mindset', they make sure to play safe in the future and they don't challenge themselves and grow their talent.

Meanwhile, when it comes to the group praised for effort, when the praise was directed at how they approached the task, how they were stretching themselves and trying something difficult by practising intensively, then it is that process of growth that they associate with admiration and value. They aren't afraid to make a mistake, because it's taking on hard things and sticking to them that they associate with praise.

The study continued. This time they gave *all* the children a really *impossible* test. Dweck observed that the group praised for effort worked harder, longer and enjoyed the test more than the group praised for their innate intelligence, even though the test was really hard. The second group got frustrated and tended to give up early.

And there was one final stage to the research. All the children were given a test as easy as the first test and asked to have another go, but the results were very different. This time, the group praised for their

How do you view your mistakes?

When someone suggests how you might do something better, do you see it as proof you're not very smart or a chance to get smarter? Your answer to this question may depend on whether you have a 'growth mindset'. Research indicates that people with a growth mindset have a brain that's better wired for monitoring their errors and for receiving the feedback that helps them improve.

intelligence performed *less well* by twenty per cent, whereas the group praised for effort *improved their performance* by thirty per cent, a staggering differential of fifty per cent in performance over three short tests and the course of their research.

Aside from Christian and his den, did we see evidence of children with an obvious growth mindset on *Secret Life*?

The answer is a resounding 'Yes'. The scientists set games and challenges of all kinds for the children and we saw the enormous appetite they had for being challenged in a supportive atmosphere in which effort was praised and tasks were as much about process as the end result. One parent of a six-year-old wrote to us afterwards and said, 'I wish they did more of this kind of thing at school – setting kids a challenge and then just leaving them alone to work through various solutions without interference from adults.'

In fact, there's research to show that we *all* have access to a bit of both mindsets – a fixed and a growth one. But if at first you don't succeed, don't give up – the children on *The Secret Life of 4, 5 and 6 Year Olds* didn't. They kept going, they tried their hardest, they learnt from their mistakes, they kept their eyes on the prize and guess what? They did it.

and finally . . .

Looking back at *all* the joyous moments from *The Secret Life of 4, 5 and 6 Year Olds* reminds us of the powerful feelings these children can evoke; they made us smile, they made us laugh, they made us well up with fellow feeling. Testament to their ability to reconnect us with some of the most important things in life – the making of a good friend, the expression of uncomfortable feelings, the challenge of sharing thoughts and ideas, the grit and resilience that pays dividends, the agony and ecstasy of winning and losing, the touching moments of jealousy, mischief, glee, shared humour, love and caring.

Beatrice: I just want to be a normal person.

There's a deep pleasure in remembering life at four, five and six, and watching these children takes us back to a simpler place. But it goes beyond mere nostalgia. We *relate* to these children at a deep level. They offer us a window onto life lived in the raw and, to our surprise and delight, we find it's not an unfamiliar place. It reminds us of situations we face every day in our grown-up lives and we find that Little People really can tell us things about Big People that can help us live our lives with more engagement, more honesty and more joie de vivre.

And just as their behaviour gives us pause to reflect on our own, so too does the way their brains are being shaped by what they are learning, and how they are wired and rewired day by day with every new experience. This fine-tuning of our brains – at a peak at this young age – continues *throughout* our lives and the children offer a stark reminder that it's never too late to unlearn an old habit and to try a spot of rewiring of our own.

We set out to find out *why* these children do the things they do and behave the way they do, and with the help of Professor Paul Howard-Jones, Dr Elizabeth Kilbey, Dr Alison Pike and Dr Sam Wass we came a little closer to understanding this critical age when the blueprint for so many of our future interactions and social skills is laid down. But in the process we saw that children have lessons for us all, and that paying attention to the way they approach life is at once very, very funny as well as good for the soul.

If you could change one thing in the whole wide world what would it be?

George: I don't know, I'm only five.

Appendix 1
The making of . . .

The question we get asked most often about the making of *The Secret Life of 4, 5 and 6 Year Olds* is how did we choose the children.

As soon as the series was commissioned in 2015 we conducted a nationwide search via Channel 4 and we sent out fliers to more than 3,500 nurseries, schools and activity centres. We also street-cast, and we used several social media platforms, from Facebook to Mumsnet.

There followed a lengthy process as we hosted group events, mini interviews, countless conversations with parents, schools and nurseries, as well as home visits. We were looking for children who captured our imagination and who would benefit from the experience of taking part.

Decisions were hard to make. We knew we wanted a well-balanced group of children, representing a broad range of personalities, abilities and backgrounds, much as you would find in any classroom in the country.

Once we had selected the children our duty of care to them and their parents cannot be overstated. Our children were too young to sign up for the project themselves so the parents agreed on their behalf. The cornerstone of our 'consent' process is that it is *ongoing*. In other words, parents are told what to expect at every stage of the project, not just in pre-production, and during the filming itself, but through the edit and right up to transmission of the finished programmes so that they are fully informed about every aspect of the series.

First we sent them a list of frequently asked questions – everything from the kinds of tasks and activities the children would be doing to how many pairs of trousers to

bring in on the day. We talked them through possible worst-case scenarios – what if their child was super shy, or played up or didn't appear to be enjoying it – and who they should speak to. Only once the entire process had been talked through at length, and once the families had been visited by an independent psychologist who approved their decision to take part, did we ask parents to sign the forms.

But our duty of care didn't stop there. The team of people looking after the children were given legal checks before filming. They included highly trained teachers and teaching assistants as well as two chaperones, who were on hand at all times to take children to the toilet and look after them at lunchtime.

And of course we talked to the children throughout the day and made sure they could tell us if they were unhappy about anything. We also talked to their parents at the beginning and end of every day, telling them what their child had got up to and detailing any big achievements or upsets, much as any school or nursery would do. And we asked parents to be alert to any signs of distress in their children during the evenings.

The children spent one or two weeks with us across the summer holidays in playgrounds and playrooms that were often far better resourced than their own schools, doing fun activities with a bunch of new friends, and it was no surprise that they rarely wanted to leave at the end of it. We wanted this to be an experience that they would cherish and to repay the enormous trust their parents had placed in us by signing them up for the series.

The other question we are often asked is how on earth we filmed it. Early on we decided that the best way to capture the children's conversations and exchanges without interrupting the flow of their play would be to use remotely operated cameras – the 'documentary rig'. During the past three summer holidays we took over an infant school and rigged the inside play space and the outside playground with about thirty cameras, plus fixed mini-cams attached to tree houses and home corners.

To really inhabit the children's secret world we needed to be in and amongst them, not peering down at them from above, and a big priority was making sure the cameras were all down at the children's eye level. We moved the height of the camera each week to respond to the new age-group coming in.

Once the cameras were in place, the challenge for the camera crew was enormous. These children had come to play. And, as anyone who's ever watched children playing knows, they barely sit still for two seconds. It required an extraordinary level of concentration from the camera operators. No sooner had you lined up a shot than the children would move on, leaving a camera focused on . . . nothing. The beauty of our camerawork lies in the extraordinary close-ups of the children's expressions, their eyes breaking into a smile, the laughter, the

emotions passing across their faces – and these shots were the hardest to get. By tuning in to each of the children and listening to them, as well as looking at the monitors, the team began to predict the way the children moved around the space and the coverage just got better and better as filming carried on.

They joy of the fixed rig is the intimacy of the footage it captures, and crucial to this was the sound. Each child was wired up with their own microphone which they kept throughout their time with us. This meant we could tune in to each one of them and follow their story. We captured every word uttered, whispered or gasped – nothing passed undetected. This is what gave us such a privileged and unparalleled window onto the innocent and secret world of these children; the highs, the lows, the humour, the unfolding drama.

If a child got upset or had a tantrum during filming we only showed it if it was justifiable in the circumstances, contextualized by our scientists, and if we were satisfied that showing it would not be harmful to the child. The well-being of the individual child was paramount at all times.

That said, our parents knew their children were not going to be little angels all day long. It was important to show the reality of life in the playground in all its brutality and humanity. It was this documentary veracity that made the behaviour so relatable to us as adults.

And it was our scientists who placed the children's behaviour within the bigger context. Physically situated at the heart of the production, with access to each of the children's individual microphones, they monitored and commented on the entire process and were often reluctant to leave their seats even to grab

a cup of tea or a bite to eat lest they missed something. This privileged access to the children's exchanges, interactions and altercations gave them the opportunity to observe and infer in a way that was unprecedented in their experience.

In three of the four series we have been supported by the Wellcome Trust and this encouraged us to film the scientists observing the children *in real time*, rather than capturing their thoughts after the event. Some of my favourite moments across the production have been seeing the scientists helpless with laughter as someone goes in for another lick of the chocolate cake, another turn of the handle of the gumball machine, another shove, another prod, another poke.

It's been just as enjoyable watching our scientists *disagree* with each other. They come from different fields – Neuroscience, Developmental Psychology, Clinical Psychology – and this fly-on-the-wall filming has allowed us to celebrate the subtle differences between these disciplines as well as their shared body of knowledge on child development.

But there was no doubting the real stars of the show. Everyone in the science room, the gallery, the art department and the production office were kept separate from where the filming was happening to keep the experience as real as possible for the children, but occasionally we would come across a Tia or an Alfie or a Beatrice in the corridor and the refrain would always be the same, 'They look so small!' We were so used to seeing our screens filled with the children's beautiful faces, their open-heartedness, their sense of mischief and astonishing social intelligence, that we were always taken aback to see them in the flesh, in their actual dimensions.

Invariably we felt in awe of them.

Appendix 2
Do try this at home

Some of the tasks featured in *The Secret Life of 4, 5 and 6 Year Olds* can be done just as well at home. Here are some that were either suggested by teachers, adapted from well-known science experiments or based on scientific research.

Making friends

Shared Resources

As a parent one is tempted to 'make sure there's always enough to go round' – enough scissors, enough pens and pencils, rolling pins. But teachers deliberately put out two glue pots for five children, two scooters for a group of children in the playground or one magnifying glass for a group of three foragers in the woods, specifically to encourage children to take turns. They call it Shared Resources. Children learn through doing and this gives the adult lots of opportunities to positively reinforce any pro-social behaviour, 'That was very thoughtful of you to let Theo have a turn.'

Cookie Drop

Several desirable biscuits are left at strategic places in a room where children are playing. There are no instructions – it's up to the children to work out what to do. This tests the children's willingness to share, their powers of reasoning and their understanding of rules, as well as their kindness and empathy. Does the finder keep them all for themselves or do they share? If they share do they do it equally or unequally? And how do they describe what happened when the adult comes back?

Little grown-ups

Adult World

We got as many real items of clothing from as many different cultures as we could find: little tuxedos, hats, veils, bridesmaid's dresses, cloaks, wigs, sunglasses, handbags, parasols, aprons, coats, shoes, masks, as well as uniforms and actual dressing-up clothes. And we put as many real items from the adult world – an old-fashioned telephone, pasta, flour, lemons, bread, etc. – in the Home Corner, plus tins in the shop, real (foreign currency) money in the till, real babies' clothes for the dolls, to encourage imaginative role play.

Language and the art of persuasion

Retell a Story

Read a story with challenging vocabulary and plot and ask a child to retell the story. How many twists and turns of the story can they remember? How many of the new words? OR learn a poem – a recent study found children better than adults at committing verse to memory.

Have a Conversation with Your Future Self

A recent study suggests that if three, four and five-year-olds are encouraged to have a five-minute chat with their future or past selves, it can help them 'time-travel' mentally and make better decisions about their own needs, like remembering not to wear their bikini outdoors in winter or to put sun cream on and wear a hat in summer.

What's the Connection?

In small groups, give children three inanimate, unconnected objects – a dustpan, a tiara and a piece of rubber pipe – and ask them to create a play that links the three items. Inspired by the Torrance Test of Creative Thinking, a classic test of imagination and inventive play.

Feelings and what to do with them

Disappointing Presents I

There are two versions of this experiment. In the first, gather together some everyday used objects – a rubber band, a tea bag, a pencil. Wrap them up and present it to a group of children as an exciting present or reward – how do they respond? Our favourite response on the programme was the boy who said his rubber band was 'cool' and immediately put it on his head and started playing with it.

Tethered

Join two four-year-olds at the wrist with a delicate paper chain and see how long they can remain attached. This game tests the children's theory of mind, their ability to compromise and negotiate, their memory, attention and ability to follow instructions.

Girls and boys

Draw Your Home

Ask boys and girls to draw their home and see whether their focus is more on the people who live in it or the design of the building. This is based on a study in which girls tended to emphasize people whereas boys focused on the architectural structure.

The Lemonade Test

A trusted adult gives some homemade lemonade to boys and girls, saying they've made it especially and not telling them it has a spoonful of salt added. Do they say it's disgusting or try to spare the adult's feelings?

Best Dressed

Challenge two boys and two girls to dress up as beautifully as they can, saying there's a prize for 'best dressed'. Take a photo. Now ask them to swap outfits. Take another photo and announce a winning pair.

Resisting temptation

The Chocolate Test

A simple variation of the classic Marshmallow Test. With shared responsibility, the children are sat at a table and each given one square of chocolate on a plate and told they can all have two squares of chocolate, but only if no one in the group eats their piece while the adult is out of the room.

Clear Rules, No Rules

Any tempting treat left out with either clear rules – Don't Touch/This is for Later – or no rules, provides a test of a child's self-control, their sense of right and wrong, and their ability to cover up with a fabricated story.

Learning to lie, learning to love

Disappointing Presents II

In this version, children are encouraged to make something themselves and wrap it up to give to a friend. How does the friend respond – do they have sufficient theory of mind yet to appreciate that someone else has put time and effort into it? Or do they toss it aside and say its rubbish?

The Sally–Anne Test

A classic test of theory of mind. Children are introduced to two puppets, Sally and Anne. Sally takes a marble and hides it in her basket. Sally 'leaves' the room and, while she is away, Anne takes the marble out of Sally's basket and puts it in her own box. Sally comes back and the child is asked, 'Where will Sally look for her marble?' If the child points to Sally's basket this shows that a child can see that Sally has her own beliefs that don't necessarily correlate with reality.

How to win at winning and losing

Pass the Parcel and Musical Statues

These children's party favourites are both great tests of emotional regulation, particularly the old-fashioned Pass the Parcel, in which it was winner takes all, no sweets for the losers.

Uneven Rewards

Different sized gold coins are given to the team leader – does the child reward their friends or the team members who did best at the task? How is it negotiated?

If at first you don't succeed . . .

Magic Carpet

Find a small rug with different patterns on each side and, in teams of two or three, challenge them to find a way to flip the rug *without stepping off it*. The key is to turn the corner of the rug, stand on the edge and slowly unfold the rest of it. A test of spatial awareness and communication.

Hold 'em Up

A simple game of determination. Each child is challenged with holding a teddy above their head for as long as they can until just one winner remains.

Stepping Stones

Three children, two planks, one box. Can the three children use the items to get from one side of a room/ garden/playground to the other without their feet touching the floor? A classic test of leadership, team work and communication skills.

acknowledgements

For anyone interested in more detail on the scientific studies referred to throughout this book, please visit www.panmacmillan.com/secret-life-references

I'd like to thank all the children who took part in the first sixteen episodes of *The Secret Life of 4, 5 and 6 Year Olds*. You each made a unique contribution. Thanks also to your parents, who took such a giant leap of faith – we appreciate the enormous trust you placed in us – this book is dedicated to your children.

The series has been more than a job to all of us who've been lucky enough to work on it. I can't begin to acknowledge everyone who's contributed to its success, but I would like to thank the following people:

The entire crew across all sixteen episodes. You know who you are – everyone from camera and sound to casting and production, to gallery team, runners, props, post, music and editorial. I am grateful to you all for the love and care you have devoted to the project.

Our wonderful teachers – Kate, Simon, Oliver, Phillippa and Zach.

Our scientists, Prof. Paul Howard-Jones, Dr Elizabeth Kilbey, Dr Alison Pike and Dr Sam Wass, for their knowledge, wisdom and good humour.

Cathy Rogers who's original idea was instrumental to the project.

Sara Ramsden, Heather, Rita, Anna and John at Channel 4 for their support and editorial rigour.

Jim Allen and all at RDF for their unerring belief in the pilot and ongoing editorial support. And to Sarah and Adrian for making the book happen.

Iain Dodgeon and Lucy McDowell at Wellcome for the encouragement to experiment.

Jonno, Tim, Nick, Annie and all at Evolutions, Nathalie at C4, Mark Johnson and Mike, Misha, Miles and Nick at RDF for the photos.

Jamie, Senior Editor at Pan Macmillan, for seeing the potential for a book straight away and steering it through so expertly. And Jo Unwin for her friendship and support.

My fellow travellers Jo, Glynis, Lavinia, Wenna, Dolly, Ezra, David, Anna Watkins and David Watkins.

And for their magical thinking, love and inspiration, Jesse, Alice and Esme, and Simon.

Teresa Watkins, August 2017